Contents

Contents

Preface

In the chapters that follow, C. L. Barber explores the creation of Elizabethan tragedy in the formative work of Christopher Marlowe and Thomas Kyd. Although only one of the plays under consideration, Marlowe's *Doctor Faustus*, is fully tragic in the sense Barber seeks to clarify, each contributes significantly to the emergence of tragedy as the most compelling form for comprehending experience in the drama of the Elizabethan stage. Because much of it was written with the crowning masterpieces of Shakespearean tragedy in mind, this extended essay on *Tamburlaine*, *Doctor Faustus*, and *The Spanish Tragedy* can also be read as a speculative inquiry into some of the enabling theatrical conditions of Shakespeare's tragic artistry. Barber illuminates what is distinctive to the action of each of these plays, but he does so by showing how each can be understood in relation to the rapid maturation of the Elizabethan theater as a "place apart" from the established institutions of church and state, to the characteristic constellations of needs Marlowe and Kyd brought to their engagement with the new professional theater, and to large historical forces conditioning author, audience, and theater in the complex social and religious circumstances of Renaissance/Reformation England.

The composition of this short book has a long and often interrupted history. When *Shakespeare's Festive Comedy* appeared in 1959, Barber had begun work on a book-length study of Marlowe, which he never published. Among the unpublished papers that came to me after his death on March 26, 1980, are parts of an incomplete book manuscript, dated 1961, entitled "Marlowe's Blasphemy and the Creation of Elizabethan Tragedy." Parts of chapters 1 and 2 of the present book were published in the mid-sixties, and a number of incomplete drafts among his papers show that he then still thought of his work on Marlowe as a book project. During that time, Barber also became increasingly preoccupied with understanding the importance of *The Spanish Tragedy*, though it would be several years before he produced a working draft for a chapter on Kyd. Although much of his thinking about Kyd was oriented toward Shakespeare's subsequent use of tragic form, particularly in *Hamlet*, Barber's work on *The Spanish Tragedy* grew out of and built on the effort to understand the "creation of Elizabethan tragedy" central to the Marlowe project.

Barber's revision and amplification of these chapters extended into the last year of his life. At that time he thought of them as parts of a larger study centered on Shakespeare's use of tragic form. But *The Whole Journey: Shakespeare's Power of Development*—unfinished at Barber's death, and left to me to complete—had by then grown into a work that was broadly concerned with all the major phases and genres of Shakespeare's art. Both the size and the design of *The Whole Journey* resisted the integration into it of Barber's studies of Marlowe and Kyd. The publication of these chapters as a separate book has proved to be a more effective way to present their distinctive contribution to an understanding of the Elizabethan theater at the moment when its extraordinary potentialities were first being realized. Their cumulative statement about the swift maturation of Elizabethan poetic tragedy provides an appropriate culmination for Barber's sustained meditation on the essential contributions Marlowe and Kyd made to the English theater.

Chapter 1 includes parts of Barber's essay, "The Death of Zenocrate: 'Conceiving and subduing both' in Marlowe's *Tamburlaine*," *Literature and Psychology* 16 (Winter 1966): 15–24.

Chapter 2 includes most of Barber's essay on *Doctor Faustus*, "'The form of Faustus' fortunes good or bad,'" *Tulane Drama Review* 8 (Summer 1964): 92–119. Chapter 3 is published for the first time. Although all three chapters were in states that Barber regarded as close to complete, each had some places, usually clearly marked, that were not in finished form. In these places, my editing has at times blurred into the work of minor revision or amplification, always done with the intent of clarifying the direction in which the text was heading. I have played a somewhat more active role in the last few pages of the chapter on *Doctor Faustus*, which, although only sketched out by Barber, contain an important clarification of his effort to articulate his complex response to a play he admired greatly but found, often, very disturbing. Whenever alterations were required to disentangle these chapters from Barber's attempt to place them within *The Whole Journey*, I have based them closely on earlier drafts.

In Barber's original plan, the book on Marlowe was to have been also a commentary on the uses of psychoanalytic thought in approaching Elizabethan theater as a complex social phenomenon grounded in its historical moment. Among his papers are a number of drafts from this Marlowe project, dating from the early 1960s, which, although unfinished, often illuminate the critical convictions and the speculative historical framework Barber brought to his work on Elizabethan tragedy. In the introduction I have attempted to represent some of the main lines of thought Barber pursued in these drafts and in another group of unfinished papers, written later, which are chiefly concerned with the place of Kyd's *Spanish Tragedy* in the development of Elizabethan drama.

In preparing these chapters for publication, I have benefited from the perceptive criticism of Peter Erickson, Stephen Greenblatt, Murray Schwartz, and Edward Snow, and from the careful work of two talented graduate assistants, Willard Rusch and Mary Soliday. Carol Neely and Jan Hinely provided illuminating responses to a draft of the introduction. I am grateful to the University of Chicago Press for its support of the project throughout. George Putnam Barber, Lucy Barber Stroock, and Robert Ennis Barber have kindly supported my efforts to see

Note on Texts

Marlowe quotations are from *The Works of Christopher Marlowe,* ed. C. F. Tucker Brooke (Oxford: Clarendon Press, 1910). Quotations from *The Spanish Tragedy* are from the Revels Plays edition of Philip Edwards (London: Methuen, 1959). Shakespeare is quoted from the Riverside edition of the *Complete Works,* ed. G. Blakemore Evans (Boston: Houghton Mifflin, 1974).

Introduction

"Art gathers in our attention," Barber wrote, "pulling it away from other things into a wholeness; but a sense of a work's place, of its author, its genre, its moment, environs and controls our enjoyment." Our own responses to the work, and the assumptions about art and life we bring with them, are part of this process, part of the work done by the work, which will invariably carry us into a region of understanding that eludes full comprehension, "because what it works on can never be fully known":

> It worked on, and for, the author, doing things for him; it worked in his time; it works for us. That the artifact exists by relation to indeterminable life precludes a conclusive account of it, however well we know it in the text or performance. Yet we experience art as a process of creation, as Paul Klee said, creation by ourselves, and by the author. So criticism, fortunately, will always be concerned with the new meanings a work takes on as our own changing sense of life leads us to see new relations "within" it. And what the work was for its author in his time is part of this constituting life and will also always concern us, even when we do not focus specifically on this dimension.

Barber's chapters on Marlowe and Kyd exemplify his conviction that the critic must be equally attentive to the work's inner integrity and to its complex interaction with the historical conditions that shape it as a process of creation. Along the way, these chapters also provide a number of telling glimpses into critical assumptions—about the resources of interpretation and about the historical context of Elizabethan tragedy—that they put into practice. As a critic, Barber clearly felt more at home enacting his conception of critical activity than in formulating it, partly, I believe, because of his sound perception that a fully engaged criticism will always embody a complexity of response that even the most subtle statements of critical method will tend to simplify or falsify. A comparable wariness about formulating general conceptions of a historical epoch, which the literary text can then be coaxed into confirming, perhaps partly accounts for the resistance he encountered in himself when he tried to give general expression to his sense of the Elizabethan moment. But he also believed it necessary to be as clear as possible about what sort of thing we are doing when we interpret a literary work and to recognize as fully as possible the contexts that shape our understanding of it.

Barber's unfinished book manuscript on Marlowe was originally conceived as a study that would provide not only an effort to comprehend what was fundmental to Marlowe's achievement but a consideration of the methodological and historical issues of literary interpretation encountered in that effort. A rather extensive array of incomplete drafts among Barber's papers—of introductions, theoretical chapters, and appendices—dramatizes the frustration he experienced when he tried to find a form adequate to both sides of this project. But these pages are thick with observations that reflect suggestively on the critical convictions and historical speculations underlying his reading of Elizabethan drama. The same is true for a group of papers connected with what became the chapter on Kyd that closes this book. Barber addressed the importance of *The Spanish Tragedy* in the development of Elizabethan drama in a series of lectures delivered at Smith College in the fall semester of 1966 in a lecture on Kyd's play and *Hamlet* presented in a Humanities Symposium at the State University of Buffalo in the spring of 1969. Among his papers are typed notes for some of the lectures given at Smith and a transcript of the lecture given at SUNY/Buffalo.

These papers also include several unfinished drafts Barber wrote while spending the academic year of 1969–70 at the Center for Advanced Study in the Behavioral Sciences at Stanford University. The papers in this last group, in which Barber had begun to think of his work on Marlowe, Kyd, and Shakespeare as a single book project, are particularly useful for their speculations on the relations of *The Spanish Tragedy* to Shakespeare's use of tragedy.

It is not feasible to reproduce these drafts here: all are either unfinished, missing pages, or superseded by later drafts; much of what they contain Barber integrated into what are now the chapters of this book; and together they are very repetitious, since they often represent new efforts to use in an altered format or perspective revised statements of ideas arrived at earlier. In this introduction I have gathered up materials—both from drafts connected with Barber's unfinished book project on Marlowe and from the later drafts centered on Kyd's achievement— which illuminate the points of orientation around which Barber's thinking about Elizabethan tragedy developed. Unless otherwise specified, all quotations are from these unfinished drafts. The papers on Marlowe that are dated give dates from 1961 to 1965, though his work on them had begun earlier and included revisions made later. Quotations from those papers primarily concerned with Kyd represent materials that range from 1965 to 1976; most of them, however, are from the drafts of 1969–70.

The possibility that I have quoted passages Barber would not have wished to see in print is, of course, substantial and regrettable. I assume full responsibility for the selections I have made, which I have regularly tested against my understanding of the development of Barber's ideas about critical method and about the historical context of Elizabethan drama. My hope is to display something of the kind of insight—about criticism and about literature—that made Barber so important a figure for those who knew him as teacher, colleague, and friend.

Abundant indications of Barber's generative influence on others reflect both the influence of his published work and the immense personal generosity of a gifted teacher and colleague. In following out the logic of his own project of long standing, Barber not only kept abreast of the most innovative work being done by others in Renaissance criticism but actively supported and encouraged younger critics who were rethinking fundamental assumptions that had long guided the interpretation of Renaissance literature. In the year of his death, the editors of *The Woman's Part: Feminist Criticism of Shakespeare*[1] provided this dedication for their collection of essays: "To the memory of C. L. Barber, with gratitude for his nurturing, demanding support of us, of other women, and of feminist criticism." In the same year, *Representing Shakespeare: New Psychoanalytic Essays,*[2] which included Barber's essay, "The Family in Shakespeare's Development: Tragedy and Sacredness," was dedicated to the "memory of C. L. Barber, who fostered so much of this work." But feminist and psychoanalytic criticism are only two of the areas whose practitioners felt themselves indebted to Barber's work and personal support, as is suggested by the remarkable variety of critical approaches represented by the festschrift for Barber edited by Peter Erickson and Coppélia Kahn.[3]

Stephen Greenblatt, in his contribution to *Shakespeare's "Rough Magic,"* points to Barber's importance as the critic

1. Carolyn Ruth Swift Lenz, Gayle Greene, and Carol Thomas Neely, eds., *The Woman's Part: Feminist Criticism of Shakespeare* (Urbana: University of Illinois Press, 1980).

2. Murray M. Schwartz and Coppélia Kahn, eds., *Representing Shakespeare: New Psychoanalytic Essays* (Baltimore: Johns Hopkins University Press, 1980).

3. In a time in which specialist anthologies, organized by particular critical methodologies, are proliferating, the editors of *Shakespeare's "Rough Magic": Renaissance Essays in Honor of C. L. Barber* (Newark: University of Delaware Press, 1985) were able to produce an exceptionally comprehensive collection of critical perspectives by soliciting essays from a varied group of distinguished writers who had one thing in common, their shared respect for and indebtedness to the work of Barber. Coppélia Kahn observes in her introduction to this volume: "This collection presents a counterpoint of critical approaches which nonetheless share a certain harmonic structure. Their diversity, and their focus on the genres of comedy and tragedy, reflect Barber's interests. Their diversity stems from the integration of traditional literary-historical scholarship with extraliterary perspectives: psychological, social and historical, feminist, deconstructive, the sort of integration which was Barber's forte as critic and teacher" (p. 15).

whose work "has most clearly taught us [that] the Elizabethan and Jacobean theater was itself a *social event.*"[4] Barber saw the theater as a social process that participated fully and reciprocally in the larger cultural and political dynamics of its historical moment. Certainly the effort to locate Marlowe and Kyd in relation to their historical moment is at the center of Barber's work in this book. And it is, I think, this dimension of his work that connects it most closely to current critical discussions of Renaissance drama.

In *Shakespeare's Festive Comedy*, Barber explored how "Shakespeare's drama can be seen as part of the process by which our culture has moved from absolutist modes of thought towards a historical or psychological view of man."[5] This study is often and, I think, rightly regarded as a work that contributed significantly toward constructing the field of inquiry now usually referred to as the new historicism. But it would be misleading to regard Barber simply as a precursor of more recent work on the historical relations of Elizabethan drama. Barber's own further work on Shakespeare, Marlowe, and Kyd, after *Shakespeare's Festive Comedy*, deepened his exploration of the place of Renaissance drama in its historical context. This work shares with new historicist writers an insistence that the literary work can only be satisfactorily known when it is placed within the cultural dynamics of its historical moment. Barber shared as well a conviction that the work of literature, as a part of the history it participated in, can illuminate the historical moment, and that, when read historically, no sharp separation can be made between the work as one sort of thing and the historical "background" as another—with the background called up to "explain" what the work means. For both Barber and the new historicism, the drama helped to shape the culture that shaped it. Barber also believed that the Elizabethan theater was animated by tensions and contradictions embedded in the very structures of Elizabethan thought and society, and that the great writers

4. "Invisible Bullets: Renaissance Authority and Its Subversion," in *Shakespeare's "Rough Magic,"* p. 295.

5. *Shakespeare's Festive Comedy: A Study of Dramatic Form in Its Relation to Social Custom* (Princeton, N.J.: Princeton University Press, 1959), p. 221.

used the theater's disruptive power to dramatize situations that question the historically dominant social and ideological orders.

There are also, however, notable points of difference between Barber's work in this area and that of critics more directly associated with the articulation of new historicist tenets—greater differences, perhaps, than those which emerge within the (hardly monolithic) field of new historicism and its (largely) British kin, cultural materialist criticism. Barber departed from much new historicist writing—sometimes in degree, sometimes in kind—in his extensive use of psychoanalysis as a mode of interpretation crucial to historical understanding; in his abiding insistence on the ultimate irreducibility of dramatic form to the drama's dynamic relations with the culture; and in his emphasis on recognizing in the distinctive and developing subjectivity of particular authors both the author's participation in the historical process and that which, in individual artistic temperaments, resists being subsumed within the historical. Though he believed that neither formal nor authorial concerns could be effectively addressed independently of historical context, he did not wish to dissolve either the formal properties of the literary text or the particular artistic development of individual authors into a master category called the historical.

Barber also believed that it was in the imaginative control it achieved through dramatic form as a unified, ironic action that the theater was able to find its place and exert its force within the complex social life of Elizabethan England. Taken together, both his emphasis on formal mastery and his way of understanding dramatic form as an agency of social awareness and social change address a problematic area that is being contested within new historicist and cultural materialist criticism. Jonathan Dollimore, in sharp contrast to Barber's insistence on the controlling power of dramatic form, believes that the "notion of structural coherence" has tended to obscure the "subversive" thrust of English Renaissance drama, and he sees the achievement of the drama instead in its "destabilising effect of dramatic *process*." He does see "some kind of closure" in this drama, but of a "perfunctory" sort; closure is the drama's enforced but superficial concession to authoritarian censorship, "a kind of condition for subversive thought to be foregrounded at all." Dollimore values the "social and political realism" of the drama, which he finds not in the overall movement of a dramatic action but in Brechtian "discontinuities" that belie formal coherence.[6] Greenblatt, on the other hand, in contrast to Barber's view of the drama as an agency of social change, sees the drama caught up in a larger social and political dynamic whereby Elizabethan authority perpetually generated voices of subversion and transgression only to recapture them for its own purposes by processes of "containment." The Elizabethan theater, named for us after a reigning queen "whose power is constituted in theatrical celebrations of royal glory and theatrical violence visited upon the enemies of that glory," repeats on the stage a theatrical process of engendering and containing subversion central to the state's authorization of its own power: "the form itself, as a primary expression of Renaissance power, contains the radical doubts it continually produces."[7]

Dollimore celebrates the drama's power to articulate fully its subversive relations to an oppressive, authoritarian ideology. Greenblatt sees in Elizabethan dramatic form an extension of the dynamic of subversion and containment basic to the recuperative practices of this oppressive ideology (and, apparently, all dominant ideologies).[8] Different as Dollimore's and Greenblatt's positions are from one another, each, I think, assumes a much more direct relationship than Barber does between the Elizabethan theater and the articulation of Elizabethan ideology. Barber is concerned neither with the capacity of the drama to confront head on, and subversively, the dominant ideology, nor with the drama's incapacity to find ways of fully extricating itself, at the level of ideology, from social and political practices it identifies as oppressive. *The Spanish Trag-*

6. *Radical Tragedy: Religion, Ideology and Power in the Drama of Shakespeare and His Contemporaries* (Chicago: University of Chicago Press, 1984), pp. 60, 63.

7. "Invisible Bullets," p. 297.

8. See the conclusion of his essay, where Greenblatt completes a line of thought that argues that we can recognize the prominence of "subversive" ideas in Elizabethan drama only because they are no longer subversive to our culture, which has evolved its own way of extending the dynamic of containing subversion that could threaten it: "And we are free to locate and pay homage to the play's doubts only because they no longer threaten us. There is subversion, no end of subversion, only not for us" ("Invisible Bullets," p. 298).

edy, in his reading, does not present a case against absolute monarchy, much less propose an alternative to such an ideology,[9] and *Doctor Faustus* does not articulate a coherent refutation of the Christian cosmos that dooms its protagonist to damnation. Nor, for Barber, is the force of these plays as social actions diminished thereby.

Barber's understanding of the theater as a social process is closer to that advanced in Louis Montrose's effort to delineate a "Shakespearean anthropology" or in Franco Moretti's attempt to place English Renaissance tragedy in a historical path that led to the English Revolution. Like Barber, Montrose sees in the work of the dramatists the creation of "a new kind of cultural space"; within that space, "character and action are not subordinated to doctrinal ends which transcend the fiction. Rather, conventional and often contradictory modes of belief and patterns of behavior are recreated within the world of the play as the manifestations of complex human characters in conflict with each other and with themselves."[10] For Barber, as for Montrose, this interplay of character and action liberates a realm of experience—responsive to the conditions of social experience in Elizabethan England—that continually tests and exceeds the adequacy of the reigning ideologies to control its reception, to fix limits on the ways in which it can be understood. As Barber notes, the moral categories of religious orthodoxy have no trouble naming Faustus's sins, but they cannot account for the heroic dimension of Faustus's quest, his responsiveness to a dimension of Renaissance experience that calls for a new sense of human possibility.

The drama, as Barber reads it, did not formulate a new ideology, or, in most instances, provide a frontal attack on an old one, but it invited new ways of understanding social experience by the very nature of the theatrical representation of experience it dramatized. By drawing on deep tensions within an age of considerable cultural dislocation, the theater could dramatize situations that provided new forms of awareness for cultural

---

9. See Barber's speculations in chap. 3 about what Brecht would have had to do to have reclaimed *The Spanish Tragedy* for Brechtian causes.

10. "The Purpose of Playing: Reflections on a Shakespearean Anthropology," *Helios*, n.s. 7 (1980): 70–71, 66.

understanding to take root in. As Moretti observes, "new ages are not brought into being merely through the development of new ideas: the dissolution or overthrowing of old ideas plays an equal part in their emergence." Moretti sees in English Renaissance tragedy "one of the decisive influences in the creation of a 'public' that for the first time in history assumed the right to bring a king to justice. . . . Tragedy disentitled the absolute monarch to all ethical and rational legitimation. Having deconsecrated the king, it thus made it possible to decapitate him."[11]

Barber did not, however, think the function of tragedy could be explained by a model that was centered solely in a process of dissolving "old ideas" to make a place for the liberation of new ones. Nor did he wish to place the drama solely in an oppositional relation to the forms of power that dominated the age. With regard to the latter, he was inclined to stress the enabling dimension of the culture from which the drama sprang. He was always aware of Elizabethan drama as a product of the Elizabethan age, a drama that could be what it was by way of its participation in larger patterns of the social life of the times. If the theater helped to create the social and political awareness that would bring an end to the age of absolutism, it was nonetheless enamored of the vision of life's grandeur it associated with royal power. And if, in liberating experience from "old ideas," the theater created a sense of new possibilities, Barber saw it as preoccupied too with what it dramatized as the destructive dimensions of such liberation. For Barber, tragedy did not achieve its mature integrity as an artistic form until it learned to comprehend the limits of human experience in relation to the imagination of human aspiration released within it. Finding an ironic balance that clarified that relationship, he believed, was at the heart of Elizabethan tragic form as an artistic and a social achievement.

Barber saw both the limits and the aspirations dramatized in Elizabethan tragedy as distinctively shaped by the age to which

11. "'A Huge Eclipse': Tragic Form and the Deconsecration of Sovereignty," in *The Power of Forms in the English Renaissance*, ed. Stephen Greenblatt (Norman, Okla.: Pilgrim Books, 1982), pp. 7–8.

the drama belonged, but he looked to a psychology created in more modern times to help understand them. In *Shakespeare's Festive Comedy,* Barber made, in the words of his subtitle, "A Study of Dramatic Form and its Relation to Social Custom." The relation of the drama to society was no less prominent in his thinking about Elizabethan tragedy, though here an emphasis on tensions in religious thought and practice and on stresses within society that were potentially disruptive of the social order occupied a place akin to that which holiday had assumed in the book on comedy. What was new, as Barber looked for ways of grasping the needs served by tragedy, was his intensified interest in the pertinence, and the limitations, of psychoanalytic findings, enough so that he came to think of his work on Marlowe as "almost as much an exploration of Freud—and related writers on psychology and anthropology—as an exploration of Marlowe and his moment."

He saw himself as "'testing' psychoanalytical ideas in the way that a student of literature can test them—against literature." Such testing involved placing the interpretive power of psychoanalytic insight within the whole context of literary creation, which was for Barber, always, essentially a social context, historically shaped. He deplored the reductive tendency of many psychoanalytic studies "to *equate* social symbolic action, in folklore, art, religion, with what psychoanalysis finds in individual neuroses." But he also believed that "there is no necessity for this reductive tendency," and observed that Freud, in his later studies of "the psychological dynamics of culture, . . . came to regard the neuroses of individuals as makeshift improvisations caused by the failing, for the individual, of the great common symbolic actions of society and religion." Indeed, one can partly account for Freud's own intense concentration on the individual's private world of dreams, memories, and symptoms by noting that the "great common structures of symbolic action were losing their hold" in the modern European culture from which psychoanalysis emerged.

Barber's position here corresponds in part to that of Peter Stallybrass and Allon White, who observe that "Freud's patients can be seen as enacting desperate ritual fragments salvaged from a festive tradition, *the self-exclusion from which* has been one of the identifying features of their social class."[12] Barber would clearly agree with Stallybrass and White that "the process of symbolization is in need of social as well as psychic explication" (p. 144), but where their emphasis is on Freud's tendency "to suppress the social terrain" (p. 153) in his pursuit of psychosexual determinants, Barber emphasizes the uses of Freud's conceptual framework for recovering the social within the psychic. Like Stallybrass and White, Barber situates himself within a project, one with a long history, that is defined on the one hand by the effort to historicize Freud, to grasp the insufficiently acknowledged shaping influence on Freud's thought of late nineteenth-century European bourgeois society, and defined on the other hand by the effort to use Freud's thought to read history, to disclose cultural patterns that can be comprehended only from the vantage point of a theory of unconscious mental life.

Barber observed that the work of psychoanalysis was never totally isolated from the larger social matrix its theory often neglected. Freud's discoveries derive from "the creation of a nonce-society of analyst and patient, for the purpose of finding symbols and attitudes which may prove viable, finally, in the larger society." In the analytic session, analyst and analysand agree to abide by a set of formal conventions that binds them together in a little society of two even as it holds in suspension, temporarily, rules for communication governing society at large. Though much psychoanalytic writing fails to articulate a range of significance beyond the individual and his private history— his past infantile experience in a family, the most durable of social institutions for late nineteenth-century bourgeois culture—Freud's work proceeds from the social institution he invented:

> Freud created a new form for experience, a new sort of a place apart. By isolating therapist and patient, with conventions that tended to free memory and desire from will and act, the psychoanalytic session provided in effect a new theater of the mind. The relation between this new place and the new human poten-

12. *The Politics and Poetics of Transgression* (Ithaca, N.Y.: Cornell University Press, 1986), p. 176.

tialities it freed for expression provides a revealing, if distant, analogy to the Elizabethan theater as I am looking at it. Freud's was another epoch-making discovery of social form for experience, . . . a situation in which, in Lionel Trilling's words, the mind reveals itself as "a poetry-making organ"[13]—and one can add, in reference to all that emerged for Freud about the transference, "a drama-making organ." By the making of what might be poetry and what might be drama, analysis can move outside or back behind the symbolic action of ordinary social life, fixed as that is in the common forms of the culture.

What seems vagrant and idiosyncratic in the symptomology of neurosis finds a social form in the analytic session that can clarify stresses engendered within the dominant social relations of the culture.

The psychoanalytic situation not only countenances the freedom that enables the work to proceed but provides the form that controls the psychoanalytic process and the interpretations based on it. "What control," Barber asked, "is available for parallel literary exploration and interpretation?" He looked toward an answer in a consideration of both what is distinctive to the "literary situation" and what binds that situation to the larger life of society. The individual work occupies a place within what Harry Levin had called the "institution of literature,"[14] which is itself a social form that always exists in dynamic relation to the powerful institutional bases of social experience. Meaning does not emerge from a work of literature in the same way that it flows from the communication between patient and analyst. But like the psychoanalytic session, literary production both participates in the social experience from which it springs and offers an experience that is set apart from other forms of social life.

Because of its roots in social experience, we must "consider the literary work not as if it were a fantasy hanging in the air but as it functioned for the author and his audience as part of the symbolic action of its historical moment." In moving from

13. "Freud and Literature," *The Liberal Imagination: Essays on Literature and Society* (Garden City, N.Y.: Doubleday Anchor Books, 1957), p. 49.
14. *The Gates of Horn: A Study of Five French Realists* (New York: Oxford University Press, 1963), pp. 16–23.

Freud to literature, we should begin "not with what is most personal about the work but what is most institutional. . . . To start interpretation with institutions is to recognize that the symbolic action of men is not conducted simply on an individual basis." We will find the work's relations to its social bases functioning even in its most fantasy-laden imagery, because "what a psychoanalyst calls fantasies are not created out of whole cloth, but are the individual's strands in the fabric of civilization which men spin and weave together."

For Barber, what was "most institutional" in relation to the understanding of *Doctor Faustus* was clear—"the Communion and the drama, the church and the theater." We can most usefully start with the Communion, Barber argued, "because Marlowe, like any man of his times, started with the Communion." The social existence of the Communion—both as "a central mystery of our heritage" and as the principal liturgical arena in which the Reformation understanding of worship defined itself against Catholic thought and practice—shaped the potential for tragic action that Marlowe could realize in the new theater. The relation Barber saw between *Doctor Faustus* and the Christian Eucharist and the importance of this relation for the development of Marlowe's art beyond *Tamburlaine* are at the heart of chapter 2. What is pertinent to emphasize here is the pivotal place Marlowe's movement from *Tamburlaine* to *Doctor Faustus* occupied in Barber's understanding of the larger development of Elizabethan tragedy. Barber argued that tensions in Elizabethan culture about relationship to divinity and worship, set loose in the theater by the disruptive action of *Tamburlaine* and made explicit in the tragic action of *Doctor Faustus*, also shaped the tragic art of Kyd and Shakespeare, in which the drive toward a sacred dimension of human experience is pursued in a fundamentally secular world.

Though the secular theater developed in considerable tension with the religious thought of the times, particularly that of the more radical reformers, it sprang from a shared historical reality. The extensive doctrinal polemics of the age expressed a massive struggle to bring this complex historical moment within the framework of religious comprehension—to master reality by subduing it to its religious significance. The theater could respond with its new freedom of expression to urgent forces pressing on the historical moment, which, from the vantage point of unified religious doctrine, could only be regarded as purely negative, as simply blasphemous. Barber believed that "the new dramatic form which Marlowe developed in *Tamburlaine* made blasphemy possible—that to make it possible was, in one sense, the function of dramatic form," one way in which the drama could be responsive to pressures working within the culture, or beneath it. In the theater, blasphemy would acquire a dimension of meaning that it could not find in religious thought and practice. "In dramatizing blasphemy, Marlowe also made it something else, a heroic enterprise. This ambiguity, irreducibly dramatic, is at the core of *Tamburlaine.*"

In the work of other dramatists of the time, "we get heroes who pursue goals like those of Marlowe's great blasphemers, . . . but they do so primarily in secular terms, through rituals of state and war. Whether one calls their pride blasphemy," Barber observed, "depends on one's frame of reference." But he also noted that there is abundant contemporary commentary that saw the heroics of theatrical protagonists as an outrage to religious piety. "The Elizabethan Puritans saw the theater as 'The very Pompes of the Divell.'"[15] And "without being a Puritan, or even a practicing Christian, one can see in Elizabethan tragedy an exploration of man's striving to be godlike; one also sees, what the Puritan neglects, a tragic recognition of human finitude. Tragedy, in this perspective, appears as an alternative to the discipline of humility in religious worship."

There is, of course, no shortage of studies that look at Renaissance tragedy from the perspective of the religious thought of the time. *Doctor Faustus* in particular has been repeatedly mapped onto the extensive terrain of Elizabethan theology. Al-

---

15. On the title page of his 1633 antitheatrical tract, *Histriomastix,* William Prynne declared "*That popular Stage-playes (the very Pompes of the Divell which we renounce in Baptisme, if we beleeve the Fathers) are sinfull, heathenish, lewde, ungodly Spectacles, and most pernicious Corruptions*" (quoted in Jonas Barish, *The Anti-theatrical Prejudice* [Berkeley and Los Angeles: University of California Press, 1981], p. 84). Barish sees Prynne's invective as the culmination of the Puritan attack on the theater that was waged with increasing ferocity throughout the sixteenth century and which finally led to the closing of the theaters in 1642 (see pp. 80–83).

though Romantic criticism "tended to see Marlowe as a whole-hearted atheist ahead of his time," much historically oriented criticism of our century, moving in an opposite direction, has tended to see *Doctor Faustus* as "fundamentally a traditional Christian play." Whereas the Romantics "usually regarded the end of *Doctor Faustus* as something forced upon Marlowe by official opinion," this more recent scholarship, noting the doctrinal consistency of Faustus's final crisis with the action it culminates, has often taken the play "as expressing a change of heart, a return to orthodoxy. Either view assumes an integrated sensibility in the author as he wrote the tragedy," whether Promethean or orthodox. Barber, by contrast, saw in *Doctor Faustus* "tragic form functioning to cope with conflicted attitudes, expressing not a single point of view but unresolved tensions—unresolved except by tragedy." To grasp what is distinctive to Marlowe's achievement we must recognize "both a freethinking Marlowe and a Marlowe who comprehended orthodoxy profoundly. One can have both precisely because Marlowe was a dramatist. His sensibility was not satisfied by his 'views.' He needed to create a new drama because other forms of expression, adjusted as they were to received attitudes, could not serve his need."

Doctor Faustus becomes, in this line of argument, what Dollimore, in his discussion of the play, calls an "interrogative text" that resists resolution into a vindication either of Faustus or of the morality structure that shapes the plot.[16] For Dollimore, the play is "not an affirmation of Divine Law, or conversely of Renaissance Man, but an exploration of subversion through transgression." He sees the force of the sacred, however, largely through its manifestation as law. What Faustus will transgress is an oppressive form of power; by the end of the play the protagonist's transgression "has revealed the limiting structure of Faustus' universe for what it is, namely, 'heavenly *power*'" (p. 118). The subversive thrust of the play is to show that "far from justice, law and authority being what legitimates power, . . . power establishes the limits of all those things." Dollimore can then see the significance of the play for the further development of Renaissance drama in its intimation of a

16. *Radical Tragedy*, p. 109.

form of thought, inaccessible to Faustus himself, which can seek to free itself from authoritarian power as a limiting structure, whether it takes sacred or earthly forms. "In transgressing and demystifying the limiting structure of his world without there ever existing the possibility of his escaping it," Dollimore writes, "Faustus can be seen as an important precursor of the malcontented protagonist of Jacobean tragedy. Only for the latter, the limiting structure comes to be primarily a sociopolitical one" (p. 119).

Such an account of *Doctor Faustus* and its relation to the subsequent drama is largely compatible with Barber's understanding of an important dimension of the play, but it does not acknowledge the dimension of the play that fascinated Barber most. Where I think Barber's reading of *Doctor Faustus* departs from Dollimore's, and from the general drift of much new historicist and cultural materialist criticism of Renaissance drama, is in Barber's insistence on the appeal of the sacred to Faustus, his desire to participate in it, which he cannot not feel at the center of his need, and which he struggles to recover in blasphemous form. Barber would agree, I think, with Dollimore's claim that Faustus's transgression is "rooted in an *impasse* of despair" (p. 112), but he saw that despair as grounded less in Faustus's sense of oppression at the hands of a tyrannous power than in his exclusion from participation in the charged sacred world he glimpses, finally, in the vision of Christ's blood in the final scene. Rather than demystify this need, the most powerful poetry in the play is animated by Faustus's effort to realize it through the action he initiates.

Certainly Marlowe was, Barber observed, "of all the Elizabethan dramatists, . . . the most preoccupied with religion and the most deeply conversant with religious thought." But to see in *Doctor Faustus* only a confirmation of Elizabethan theology—or, for that matter, only a repudiation of it or an escape from it, or, in Dollimore's terms, a subversion of it—is to miss precisely "the significance of the Elizabethan poetic drama." "Religious categories current in his age and available to criticism in ours are so inclusive, on their own terms, that it is possible to fit everything in *Tamburlaine* and *Faustus* into them—except, to put it simply, the *poetry*, the realization of new human energy by the actor using poetry on the stage." And to leave this di-

mension out of account is to miss not only the heroic stature of
Faustus's "sense of the high possibilities of secular life, which
was what his nineteenth-century sympathizers chiefly saw," but
also something still "more fundamental: Marlowe's power to en-
dow the secular with a religious numen, his essentially unstable
appropriation of the divine for the human."

Marlowe's "essentially unstable appropriation of the divine
for the human" puts us very near the center of Barber's understanding of Elizabethan tragedy in its historical moment. Tamburlaine's self-worship, in which all are invited to join, gives
way to the ironies that contain Faustus's blasphemy in a tragic
action—but Faustus is a hero as well as a sinner because in his
blasphemy he seeks a demonic equivalent for the sacred experience he feels is beyond his reach. Marlowe's movement beyond
Tamburlaine to the more inclusive tragic mode of *Faustus* out-
lines a pattern consistent with the larger development of Elizabethan tragedy. The *explicitly* religious framework of *Faustus* is
essential to the imaginative design of that play, but not to the
larger development. Hieronimo's desperate need to make a religion of his lost son in *The Spanish Tragedy* looks toward Hamlet's
struggle to recover relationship to the divine in his dead father's
ghost. Both *The Spanish Tragedy* and *Hamlet*, like *Tamburlaine*,
are profoundly disruptive uses of the theater; in releasing heroic, aggressive energies beyond the control of ironic perspective, they situate their protagonists at an unstable boundary between the sacred and the demonic (which the criticism of these
plays has typically tried to resolve by locating these figures in
one category or the other). *King Lear* and *Macbeth* achieve the
perfect tragic poise of irony and compassion, balancing our response to the outrageous aggression released through sacred
or demonic investments in self and other against our awe and
sympathy for the full and poignant humanity the protagonists
dramatize even as they are alienated from it by their drive to
exceed it. The dramatic structure of these plays, like that of
Doctor Faustus, comprehends both what is heroic in the protagonists' need to transgress human limitations in the direction
of sacred or demonic fulfillment and the dreadful destruction
that the pursuit of that need through human actions and objects
entails.

"One can see the whole of Elizabethan tragedy as presenting the destructive, ironic failure of human efforts 'to gain a deity.'" But the pertinence of this view holds only insofar as "one recognizes that the tragedy works in its own ways, by its own dynamics, which are not those of religious discipline, let alone moral exhortation. The hero arrives at blasphemy by being human, otherwise we would not follow him into it; poetry conveys the thrust by the life-enhancing force of metaphor and symbol; the jealousy and cruelty of the audience, as well as its righteousness, are appealed to in leading it to ironic recognition of human limitation; cruelty, righteousness, and compassion blend ineffably in the auditors as the drama moves them from participation in a life through a death."

The dramatic, ironic control that Elizabethan tragedy learns to exercise over the energies it releases is a social phenomenon, just as the motives that animate it are rooted in a social situation. To get at this dimension of the theater, Barber was following "the tradition of literary studies in the light of comparative religion and anthropology, which comes down from Frazer through Gilbert Murray, Jane Harrison, Francis Cornford, to American critics, some partisan and polemical, like Herbert Weisinger and Stanley Hyman in his early works, others, notably Kenneth Burke and Francis Fergusson, who make use of the anthropological approach as one among several modes of understanding of the function of culture." But Barber's reading of anthropology and anthropologically informed criticism kept coming back to Freud. He found in Freud's exploration of larger cultural phenomena, from *Totem and Taboo* on, a valuable mode of access to religious worship (and artistic expression), despite Freud's own nineteenth-century scientist's scorn for religious thought: "the whole thing is so patently infantile," Freud concluded, after a summary discussion of how childhood attitudes toward the parents shape conceptions of divine figures.[17] For Barber, the continuities Freud saw in debunking the illusory character of religious formations provided a key to the sort of mature control that a traditional religious society could impart

17. *Civilization and Its Discontents, The Standard Edition of the Complete Psychological Works of Sigmund Freud*, ed. and trans. James Strachey, 24 vols. (London: Hogarth Press, 1953–74), 21:74.

to its members through its doctrines and particularly its forms of worship. Barber likened the failures of individuals who fall prey to neurotic or perverse behavior to misplaced forms of worship, investments in others, or parts of others, of needs that in a religious situation are taken up out of society and into relationship with the sacred.

Freud, who "began as a student of desire, . . . became in effect a student of worship, including unconscious worship, as his explorations led him to recognize how worship shapes, blocks, and transforms desire." But though Freud's work "greatly illuminated the dynamics of religious need and the delusions of diabolisms, his attitude toward religion functioning as an institution remained reductive." This reductive orientation, Barber believed, kept Freud from "recognizing the positive realities of worship" within the institutional framework through which a society constructs and affirms its distinctive sense of reality. In order to "correct the Freudian perspective on religion, . . . we must recognize that the discipline of religious worship can serve, in an intact communion, not the return to the infantile, but the control of infantile tendencies, their transformation into worship validating society."

The shift of emphasis Barber thus pursued did not, certainly, dismiss or neglect the importance of infantile factors, regressively enacted in response to adult situations of crisis, as psychoanalysis had come to understand them. His reading of *Doctor Faustus* derives much of its strength from his responsiveness to the ways in which infantile themes increasingly dominate Faustus's language and thought as the terrible logic of the hero's desire alienates him further and further from the social matrix of the human community. But the hero's "regression" is part of the larger design of a play that comprehends both what is common and what is distinctive to infantile attitudes, religious practices, and blasphemous defiance. And Faustus's alienation can only be fully tragic if what he is alienated from has a logic of its own, by means of which individual need, social structure, and the "discipline of religious worship" can serve, ideally, to validate one another.

In trying to understand *Doctor Faustus* and cope with Freudian insights about the motives it presents, I have been gradually forced,

over a period of years, to recognize that the tragic aberration presented in the play implies a norm which is beyond Freudian definition, . . . Looking at *Tamburlaine* and *Doctor Faustus* together,
it has seemed to me that one can understand the motives they
dramatize—and the motive for them—as a version of the Oedipus
complex. But to comprehend the perspective on the motive
which Marlowe arrives at when he achieves the balance of tragic
form, one must recognize the possibility, which hovers over
Faustus, of the resolution of the Oedipus complex in religious
fulfillment, making it the form through which a child's worship
can develop into a man's. This was not, clearly, what happened to
Marlowe as a man. As we have said, it was not the institution of
religion but the institution of the drama by which he achieved
what control he did achieve.

What is important to note here is that by following Barber's
attempt to work through and beyond a Freudian vantage point
in addressing cultural phenomena, we can see him identifying
those contexts that through their interrelationship shape his
understanding of a literary work: the larger social and cultural
matrix within which, in the case of *Doctor Faustus,* religion is
especially prominent; the institution of literature, in this instance Elizabethan theater and the development within it of poetic tragedy; and the individual temperament of the artist, particularly as the artist's power of development is revealed by a
succession of works, as in the movement from *Tamburlaine* to
Faustus. The action of *Doctor Faustus* is shaped by a cultural
situation that found directly religious expression in the great
Tudor controversy over the Mass and the status of the Communion, and that reflected the profound shift in man's relationship
to the sacred as articulated by the Reformation. But the action
is played out in a theater, an institution that occupies a very
different place from that of the church in the larger structure of
society, its values, beliefs, and activities. And finally, the play
enacts what is specific to Marlowe's response to the Elizabethan
experience and to his powers of using language and gesture and
dramatic structure, at one moment in his particular career, in a
theater he shares with others.

The special density of Barber's criticism partly derives from
his effort to keep each of these contexts in view and in dynamic

relation with one another. In coming to know a work, none of these contexts is knowable apart from the others, and none carries a kind of privileged certainty against which the others can be measured. Barber's practice is thus both circumspect and, to a degree, circular, or better, circulatory; it moves incessantly from one frame of reference to another, because each can only be understood in the context of the others. At times it nearly buckles under the pressure generated within it to say everything at once, to make simultaneously present all that we need to hold in balance if we are to grasp the whole object, the whole process, encountered in the literary text.

Barber meets the protean expansiveness of literary creation with a critical style that pursues comprehensiveness through intensely concentrated, mutually qualifying statement. In Marlowe's plays "we can see the theater being used . . . to serve and cope with motives which it is hard to name as such—motives which one cannot call religious, but which religion might have satisfied for another temperament, living through another institution, the church rather than the theater." Partly these motives are specific to Marlowe, who "achieved tragedy, I think we can see, out of a desperate need." "Because he achieved expression, we can see into his motives for it." Marlowe's need for tragic expression, however, is not knowable for us in isolation, nor could it have been realized in purely private circumstances. Marlowe had "great artistic powers to put in the service of his temperament," but these powers required for their realization "an established theater with skilled actors to whom he could give voice, and audiences willing and able to participate in his imaginings." The eagerness of these audiences for Marlowe's work makes it clear that in meeting his own need in the theater he met the needs of others as well. "The creation of a new art form, indeed, any fundamental artistic innovation, clearly must spring from needs which the culture cannot otherwise satisfy." Yet it is in the culture that the artist must find the resources that "enable, though not determine, his heroic innovation. The three great shaping factors of Marlowe's civilization, creating the need and making possible its fulfillment, were of course the church, the state, and the theater. . . . Out of his quite special relations with the three, Marlowe made an art which could put him (and his auditors) in a new relation to reality, the reality expressed in heroic tragedy."

Barber did not underestimate the problematic complexity of his approach to Elizabethan tragedy through the culture's, and the artist's, need for it. "To talk about this need apart from the work which fulfills it is difficult, and inevitably involves speculative constructs. One must make general assumptions about how culture and human nature interact and make inferences about the particular humanity of the individual artist in question." His aim, however, was not to introduce a new set of critical theories, but to call for more self-conscious exploration of assumptions and inferences we necessarily make in our whole response to literature as a process of creation and which shape our interpretation of literature whether we attend to them explicitly or not. "I think it is fair to say that we all do this, in an informal, intuitive way, whenever we read deeply in an author's work—when we read an author, not just a work. Our sense of the need for artistic achievement is part of its meaning for us: who reads Milton's epic without a sense of the blind Milton dictating *Paradise Lost* in the Restoration, *achieving* epic?"

Neither did he underestimate the complexity of the whole social situation that enabled the commercial theater to flourish in Elizabethan England. The social, economic, political, intellectual, and cultural life of what we have come to think of as the English Renaissance makes the Elizabethan theater possible. Barber's emphasis on the Reformation side of this experience derived partly from his special concern with Marlowe and *Doctor Faustus*, where the religious framework is uncharacteristically prominent, but more crucially from his special concern with tragedy, the dramatic form in which something akin to the ultimate ground for experience that religion seeks to provide is sought in relations that are outside orthodox religious worship. The great tragedies, as Barber saw them, enact destructive and self-destructive efforts to achieve total, all-or-nothing investments of self in human objects, which, because they are human, cannot sustain the immensity of need, the absoluteness of demand, brought to them.

The Reformation dismantled much of the Catholic apparatus of worship in order to isolate the individual worshiper in direct rapport with God through faith. That the old religion had for various reasons, only some of which were directly religious, failed to meet the needs of many in the sixteenth century is a basic cultural fact of the age. But Reformation thought, in promising a new relationship to the sacred, also put worshipers at risk in new ways. In areas where the Reformation triumphed, extraordinary anxiety could be generated by the absolute importance conferred upon the individual's faith in the grace of a God no longer accessible through the ritual work of the church, and whose eternal wrath toward those not saved was beyond the mitigation both of the church and of individual action.

The reformers' emphasis on the faith of the individual worshiper was met by a comparable emphasis on the individual in Renaissance thought, but here the individualistic stress was on secular achievement and advancement, on worldly power and pleasure, or on a spirituality that exalted in the human mind's potential for godlike mastery of the world. We can see an extreme development of this polarity, one which shapes Marlowe's art in *Tamburlaine* and *Doctor Faustus*, if we set the reformers' insistence on the individual's absolute dependence and subservience before God's might against the Hermetic strand of humanist thought, in which the individual was invited to attain in magic something like divine extension through the operations of his own mind. With *Tamburlaine*, Marlowe used the theater as a kind of magic; with *Doctor Faustus* he found in "the art of magic and the figure of the magician, . . . material which he could animate so as to express, within the play, what in *Tamburlaine* he had been trying to do by means of the play." By making the "search for magical omnipotence into a heroic endeavor," Marlowe enabled Faustus to become "what the hero of the Faust-book could never have been, a mythic prototype for the modern imagination. Yet at the same time the blasphemy of the Faustian sense of power is held in the rigorous ironic perspective of traditional religious understanding." The hero's total situation is open to the whole complexity of the age. "We can see Marlowe's hero as a man who in a Calvinist despair of God attempted to flee from 'the Reformation' into 'the Renaissance.' But of course Reformation and Renaissance were never really separate, at least not in England. Marlowe's play expresses, by properly dramatic means, how the two tendencies interpenetrated."

To look hard at Marlowe's crucial role in the formation of Elizabethan tragedy, however, is to see also what in Marlowe's distinctive temperament is alien to the larger development, particularly as it reaches its fullest expression in Shakespeare's work.

Marlowe's mastery of classical and theological studies, his sophisticated contemporary interests, speculative and historical, his predominantly male-oriented sensibility, even his place of birth, Canterbury, make it natural to think of him as a spoiled priest— or better, a spoiled prelate. Had he been born before the Reformation, and with the right luck, he might have found a priestly identity in experiences of the power of God and gone on to become an expert, a Pandulph, in manipulating secular ambitions and appetites in the service of the power of the Church. The Reformation and the Renaissance both worked against such a congenial destiny. The new, direct relationship with God "asked [him] hard questions, made [him] wish to die"[18]—or need to save himself by passing out vicarious death. The new theater gave the Promethean opportunity which the artist embraced, but which did not save the man.

"If Marlowe was in this extended sense a 'religious,'" Barber wrote, "Shakespeare was, clearly, a 'secular.'" Barber found "Kyd's sensibility and sense of values more Shakespearean than Marlowe's," because more "civic and familial."

Barber thought it possible that Marlowe's profound alienation from any investment of himself, through his drama, in the ongoing concerns of social life and in the values by which his society recognized its social ideal might partly reflect the "deracinating circumstances of his low birth and high education." Though Kyd was apparently born in London and Shakespeare in Stratford, both were the sons of rising men. Shakespeare would extend his father's middle-class heritage and redeem his

18. W. H. Auden, *Poems* (London: Faber and Faber, 1930), p. 77. Auden's line, which Barber apparently was quoting from memory, reads: "Found they no answer, made them wish to die."

father's economic fall by amassing his wealth in what became for him the highly profitable business of putting on plays for the public theater. Kyd centers his *Spanish Tragedy* on a respected, educated figure of middle-class propriety, a man of rising fortunes, serving the royal house capably and loyally, a grander version, perhaps, of the type of man the dramatist would have known in his father, "Francis Kidd, Citizen and Writer of the Courte Letter of London."[19]

Shakespeare found in the theatrical enterprise "a kind of security that Marlowe and Kyd never had," and his success in it reflects the theater's complex social position. Deep ties to royalty and aristocracy provided the theater with its right to exist, with a vital part of its audience, and, for Shakespeare, with most of its subject matter. But the theater chiefly sustained itself by way of its own vigorous, entrepreneurial thrust into the London entertainment market. Barber regarded this "double attitude" or allegiance as basic to the Elizabethan theater and recognized its importance at the heart of Shakespearean drama. Shakespeare's plays accepted and represented "the structural hierarchy of his society [with] its focus on the aristocracy and the court, while his rising fortunes are based in a new joint stock company and his art in a new, unprecedented special place apart." But considerable stresses were built into the relations between the traditional, organic, hierarchical ideal that structured society and the interests of those classes caught up in shifting configurations of economic and political realities. In *The Spanish Tragedy*, tensions between traditional, hierarchical society and the aspirations of the class from which Kyd himself derives are brought into the center of the violent action.

This action is ignited when, by taking first one lover and then another from the ranks of the upper middle class, the King's niece frustrates plans for a dynastic marriage. When the second of these lovers, Horatio, is murdered, the traumatic force of this murder is registered chiefly in the response of Horatio's father, Hieronimo. But prior to the murder, Kyd sets

19. From the 6 November 1558 record of Thomas Kyd's baptism at St. Mary Woolnoth in the City of London; quoted by Philip Edwards in his introduction to the Revels Plays edition of *The Spanish Tragedy* (London: Methuen, 1959), p. xviii.

in motion a "developing rhythm of social life" in the courtship of Bel-imperia and Horatio. He puts the daring, illicit lovers, and not their royal opposition, "on the side of ongoing social life." Kyd makes Horatio's affair with Bel-imperia consistent with his sympathetic presentation of the young man as a hero back from the war, as a loyal friend, and, especially, as "our Knight Marshal's son" (1.2.76), the appropriate object of his admirable father's pride and hope. A whole social dynamic is developed which links together the amorous courtship, Hieronimo's investment in the familial bond, and Hieronimo's status as a loyal, worthy servant of the state, and which is, for Hieronimo, suddenly shattered by Horatio's murder. For Barber, "the intensity of Hieronimo's motive (and our sympathy for him) is a conversion of the social energy frustrated by the murder." If "Kyd did not give body and force to this larger and prior context, as the dynamic basis for a paternal piety consistent with his fine old man's social piety, the wrong Hieronimo suffers would be merely individual, whereas the play makes it a wrong which brings into question the whole social process."

What is important in light of the further development of Elizabethan tragedy is the way in which the situation of *The Spanish Tragedy* is focused, through Hieronimo's desperation, on the violent rupture of what is initially dramatized as the harmonious integration of individual need and a functioning, legitimate, high-minded social order, centered in the Spanish king. "When we consider Hieronimo's special status as a civil servant, who arrived through the law to high but limited place at court, it is possible to read *The Spanish Tragedy* as on one side a play of social protest, on behalf of this class against the ruthless exclusiveness of the higher caste of nobility, declined from the moral responsibility of the older generation to the Machiavellianism of the new younger sort." But when we look at how Hieronimo's grief and his subsequent action call into question the legitimacy of the larger social process, we can see that "the same thing is true, in a more complex way, in *Hamlet*," where class or caste opposition is not important. In *Hamlet*, the legitimate social order is, from the outset, already shattered, visible only in the prince's doomed longing to recover the heritage of his dead father and in the sense of lost potential that defines his own place in a corrupted world. But in both *The Spanish Tragedy* and *Hamlet*, the "protest" is directed against a society that offers the protagonist no legitimate means to engage a problem of overwhelming proportions engendered within it.

In each play, revenge carries the burden of the aggression generated by the hero's alienation. But "the specific 'revenge code' (or convention), even the demand for particular justice, does not alone provide adequate terms to convey the dynamic conversion of social into individual response which the dramatists present." *The Spanish Tragedy* and *Hamlet*—in representing society's catastrophic failure, in a situation of intense crisis, to sustain the protagonist's need to know himself through his investment in society—point to a much wider range of tragic theater than the revenge play tradition. "Shakespeare makes the distinction between the simple code of revenge and the problem Hamlet confronts by the contrasting figure of Laertes," whose wild rhetoric of revenge is centered wholly in avenging his father's death, with none of the larger sense of social tradition as the matrix for individual identity that so complicates the fate of the prince:

> To hell, allegiance! vows, to the blackest devil!
> Conscience and grace, to the profoundest pit!
> I dare damnation. To this point I stand
> That both the worlds I give to negligence,
> Let come what comes, only I'll be reveng'd
> Most throughly for my father.
>
> (4.5.132–37)

Dramatizing a comparable disjunction between the deeper social problem and the limited resources of his protagonist to address it in *The Spanish Tragedy*, "Kyd makes the distinction by showing us the civic, law-abiding, pious Hieronimo becoming, in effect, a Laertes."

What Barber saw as important about *The Spanish Tragedy* for the "understanding of the function of tragic form" was not so much that Kyd "created the first great figure of the desperate, distracted revenger, but that he also dramatized the process by which a worthy, moral man, a pillar of society, becomes such a revenger." In the opening scenes, Kyd "shows us a Hieronimo whose investment of loyalty to society is consistent with his investment in his son. The crucial shift, which Kyd puts right at the center of the play, comes when in response to outrage, the larger investment is called in, so to speak, and totally invested in the dead son on the one hand and hatred for the son's murderers on the other."

In *The Spanish Tragedy*, as in *Hamlet*, "there is a crisis in the transmission of heritage which leads to the protagonist's embracing the revenge motive." In both instances, "the incommensurateness of society with the protagonist's need" provokes a kind of "'regression' from society to family." "The more inclusive dynamic structure is alienation from the extended social and religious pieties, the allegiances which maintain and validate community, in favor of total investment in a family relationship. Hieronimo's piety for his lost son matches Hamlet's for his father: in other tragedies we see comparable investments in daughters (*Lear*), in a mother (*Coriolanus*), in a wife (*Othello*). The identity of the protagonist, his sense of himself, indeed his ability to survive, comes to be focused totally on a particular family relationship." Instead of providing religious resolution for a crisis that is brought on by the failure of the social and political structure, tragedy dramatizes the protagonist compulsively investing himself in a secular, familial bond that takes up the psychic space religion might have occupied. The family bond, in taking on a quality of something like holiness, a dedication of the self to a human object of ultimate importance, provides a (tragic) alternative to religious piety.

The result, in *The Spanish Tragedy* and in *Hamlet*, is a "new, obsessive piety centered on the lost son or father." The wayward movement of the plot, shaped by the difficulties that obstruct the revenge motive, represents "the revenger's bafflement in being unable to bring his narrow piety and loathing into relationship with society." In Kyd's play, the split between the original investment in society and family and the reinvestment in the obsessive family bond "is developed very deliberately: Hieronimo is shown moving from initial pleas, laments, and demands for justice, through a crisis where public right goes on while private wrong is ignored, to the final decision, explicitly formulated, not to wait for God to do justice but to execute what Bacon called 'the wild justice' of revenge."[20]

Hieronimo's revenge, got by means of staging a play-within-the-play in which the characters acting their parts really kill one another, culminates the pressure of frustration that has earlier been released into language. Language must carry the force of a need for expression that attends the failure of society to meet the need the protagonist brings to it. "The situation of the avenger, alienated and for the time being helpless, is conveyed by the poetry of heroic adversity and the poetry of desperate delusion where, in response to the need for expression, the angry spirit distorts or projects reality so as to make it express or confirm his need."

Kyd's dramatization of the pressure toward magical thinking in situations of desperation links him more closely to Shakespeare's use of the theater than Marlowe's. "Marlowe pioneered direct, aggressive theatrical magic where vaunt becomes deed, prophesy performance; Kyd's remarkable play first exploits magical expectation as desperate or mad delusion. *Tamburlaine* presents outrageous action 'conceiving and subduing both' a latent suffering; Kyd's play and *Hamlet* begin with suffering and move to outrageous action. The outrageousness is theatrical in many figurative ways: both Hieronimo and Prince Hamlet repeatedly perform 'actions that a man might play' under the pressure of the need to express 'that within which passes show' (*Ham.* 1.2.83–84)." In both *The Spanish Tragedy* and *Hamlet*, this pressure toward expression is joined to "a drive to go beyond the theatrical to the actual, a striving to make acting turn into action. Hamlet's play-within-the-play has actual consequences in catching the conscience of the king; Hieronimo's, in the actual killing of his son's murderers." Of course, even in *The Spanish Tragedy*, Hieronimo's play-within-the-play does not reach out beyond the theatrical fiction that *is* the play. But there is a "moving down from one mimetic level to another, from the fiction of the play-within-the-play to the fiction of the play at a literal level." And what we can see in this movement "is a ver-

---

20. "Of Revenge," *Selected Writings of Francis Bacon*, ed. Hugh G. Dick (New York: Modern Library, 1955), p. 15.

sion of what I am calling theatrical aggression in which the actor, so to speak, walks across the footlights and stabs the grand duke."

The play, in releasing aggression generated by deep conflict in the society from which it derives, enacts the impulse to turn that aggression back against society. In Kyd's play, such aggression is generated structurally by the conflict between the brutality of caste interests in Lorenzo and the interests of the rising class represented by Hieronimo's investment in his family; it is enacted in the play Hieronimo stages for his royal audience, which destroys the entire royal line. Shakespeare's plays do not dramatize this conflict as such, nor do they directly criticize or repudiate social assumptions built into the aristocratic norm. But the institutional base Shakespeare finds in the commercial, public theater enables him aggressively to explore the world of court and aristocracy from a vantage point outside it; his tragedies enact self-destructive aggression generated within a society that attempts to ground itself in the royal and aristocratic ideal.

Learning to control theatrical aggression with dramatic form was, for the Elizabethan theater, an exercise in understanding its own, potentially disruptive, place within society. The limitation of *The Spanish Tragedy*, as Barber understood it, was in Kyd's failure to sustain into the play's finale the exceptionally acute social perspective developed by the earlier action, which places Hieronimo's derangement in relation not only to the ruthless dynastic interests of Lorenzo but also to the larger social ideal, centered in the beneficent king, which has served Hieronimo as well as he has served it. Hieronimo's imagination, bent on revenge and constricted to the religion he has made of his lost son, takes over the entire closing action, leaving room for no larger dramatic, ironic perspective to be developed on it. Barber found that in the Elizabethan theater "an enormous thrust toward making the imaginary real goes with a complementary pathos that the imaginary is not so." In *The Spanish Tragedy*, the theatrical aggression of the drive toward enactment is not balanced by the complementary "reflection that a poor player merely struts."

The limitation of *The Spanish Tragedy*, however, puts in high relief its distinctive strengths and enables us to see in the development of its action an "object lesson" in Elizabethan drama. "In the process of showing Hieronimo's transformation, Kyd's play gathers up moral and spiritual force and dedicates it to theatrical aggression concluding with an orgiastic enactment of omnipotence of mind." This movement in *The Spanish Tragedy* can help bring out what is most powerful, and most disruptive, in the action of *Hamlet,* though in that play "the crucial theatrical aggression is not arranged by the protagonist but by the playwright: the apparition of the ghost is perhaps the most disruptive instance in all dramatic literature of the actualization of omnipotence of mind." For the authors of both plays, "to animate the possibility of omnipotence of thought opens up channels of feeling normally closed, putting man in a new relation to experience." With the opening of such channels of feeling, making them available for the drama, the new institution, the Elizabethan public theater, could free itself from traditional ways of framing human experience, institutionalized by church and state, and make its vital, historical contribution to a new understanding of human possibility.

Barber believed the social dynamics of the drama "take us outside the 'psychological,' where the psychological is assumed to mean, as in most psychoanalytic formulations, the internalized dynamics of the constellation of the family." But with his emphasis on magic and his use of the concept of omnipotence of mind to illuminate the place of Elizabethan drama in its cultural moment, Barber was again drawing on psychoanalysis as a critical resource. Magical thinking, for Freud, is rooted in the psychic omnipotence that belongs to very early stages of infantile development, when the satisfaction of a wish appears first to be brought on by the wish itself, and later by words and gestures the child learns to associate with the fulfillment of the wish. Gradually the parents will come to take on the status of omnipotent figures, all-providing and, potentially, all-denying, on whose grace the child is wholly dependent. Processes of maturation eventually enable the child to distinguish between the satisfaction of the wish and the environment on which it depends, and to recognize the limitations of parental figures who have inherited omnipotent powers the child originally seemed to possess. But these processes never eradicate the tendency of the unconscious mind to equate the wish with its satisfaction and, by extension, thought with action, word with deed, fantasy with actuality—including fantasies of omnipotent successors to the child's early images of the parents.

The notion of omnipotence is of course crucial to religious thought and experience. Religious piety surrenders to divine agencies attributes of omnipotence that enter into psychic life with a child's earliest relations to his parents. "The Communion service, from this standpoint, can be understood as a way of releasing a man from the need to be a god and the need to make gods of parents and their substitutes." As in the infant's earliest relation to the all-providing parent, "so in the Lord's Supper it is by the mouth that the deity is approached. This is still the childlike mode of communication, potentially perverse. But for the successful communicant it is not perverse, because the object has been changed: its object *is* everything, understood now not as the parents but as the source of all being."

Communion, when it is "successful" in the terms Barber specifies, frees the human object from the need to be everything for the worshiper, as the parents once were for the child, and as Lear, leading Cordelia off to prison (and her death), expects his beloved daughter to be for him in his great age. But any experience that enhances a person's sense of his own powers, that frees pride from a perception of dependence and helplessness, will tend to ally itself to some degree with the human subject's enduring unconscious assumption of psychic omnipotence. The heady instability of sixteenth-century social experience facilitated an acting out of the drama of omnipotence of mind versus human limitation in myriad ways. For the devout reformer, what was surrendered in the extreme insistence on man's utter helplessness to determine his spiritual fate, or to have it determined for him by the intervention of the church, could be recovered by the conviction that God, in his omnipotence, promised eternal salvation for the faithful elect. What we think of as "Renaissance" thought tended to put fantasies of omnipotence in a more direct alignment with individual achievement, pursued in a world that seemed to have expanded radically the scope of secular possibilities. The prospect of a godlike extension of the human mind offered by Hermetic magic was one Renaissance phenomenon that actualized with particular directness

"the deeply rooted presumption all men have of possible omnipotence. That the realization of this presumption became a
possibility in art of course reflected and expressed new possibilities felt by the Renaissance in secular life."

In the theater, this presumption shaped the historical moment's fascination with the role of the hero and fueled the explosive new development of heroic poetry in the drama. "It was
in *Tamburlaine*, together with Kyd's *Spanish Tragedy*, that heroic
poetry was first brought into vital relation to stage action. The
effect was like magnesium thrown into water—enormous energies were released, for the theater became a place, apart from
ordinary limitations, where it was possible to dramatize radical
defiance and to mime omnipotence." In these "two great seminal plays of the decade of the 1580s," the heroic drive toward
the realization of omnipotence of mind subdues the action to
itself. "Kyd presents the anguished loss of faith in divine justice
moving through mad assertion of the omnipotence of mind to
the taking over by the revenger of the divine role; the play ends
in his actualization of vengeful fantasy by making a play turn
into real life—and then silence. *The Spanish Tragedy* thus arrives through suffering and madness at the usurpation of divinity which in *Tamburlaine* is presented as a triumphant, deliberate aggression."

Although Tamburlaine and most of the heroes in Marlowe's
"overtly blasphemous plays" are "self-making men" (the exception is *Edward II*), the "magical conception of kingship" in
Tamburlaine provides an important link to the dramatization of
omnipotent expectations that Elizabethan tragedy characteristically associated with the figure of the king. "A king can be
exalted beyond the human condition without overt blasphemy;
there was the cult of the crown in which all levels of society
joined." There were also conflicting attitudes toward kingship
among Elizabethans, notably the "basically Christian view,
nourished by the literature of the fall of princes, and the new
absolutist and divine right thinking." But what especially concerned Barber were "the magical and potentially blasphemous"
qualities which are given to kingship in the Elizabethan drama
when it comes into its own. "The great drama deals with the
subjectivity of kingship in a new way. Before it, kings were for
the most part conceived from the outside, whether as figures of

majestic authority, arbitrary power, or tyrannical violence. But after Marlowe's poetry of magical expectation has been created, the way is open to make kings the protagonists in the universal human effort at omnipotence."

Shakespeare, of course, is the dramatist who pursues this direction most fully. "King Lear in the storm is the very summit of the poetry of magical expectation and command which Marlowe initiated. . . . The figure of the king, as Shakespeare handled the idea of kingship, became the protagonist for experiments in the universal human effort at omnipotence, experiments in which Shakespeare respected the universal limits of man. For his kings want, in their large way and under the complex conditions of their office, the same things other men want—in Lear's case, the whole love of his daughters, especially his favorite daughter."

Shakespeare realizes in his art dramatic possibilities released into the theater by Marlowe and Kyd in *Tamburlaine* and *The Spanish Tragedy*. But both these plays, "in opening up new possibilities for art, trespass on the limits of art." In them, the action serves more to extend than clarify or control the impulse toward magical thinking it releases. "The artistic limitations of *Tamburlaine* are concomitants of its overriding, rather than expressing, an underlying ambivalence toward authority and divinity." In *Doctor Faustus* Marlowe brings magical possibilities under the control of tragic form. "The magic of *Doctor Faustus* . . . explicitly linked aspiration for a dominion stretching as far as the mind of man with attitudes toward authority and the need for worship." In *Faustus*, the protagonist's quest to actualize omnipotence of mind is separated from the author and subjected by the author to the resistance that the individual's presumption of omnipotence encounters in the political and religious institutions of a social world. The tragic action "enacts the blasphemous, infantile wish and at the same time demonstrates its impossibility."

Opposition to Faustus's quest for magical dominion does not, however, simply reflect the moral imperatives of a social order separate from him, or from his creator, and it is not exerted in a simple antagonism to the hero's desire. Nor does the tragedy, seen as an "alternative to the discipline of humility in religious worship," merely duplicate the moral lessons of the church in theatrical form. "Control by tragic form, as against control by moral principle, works, I believe, by fulfilling motives, carrying them through to their destructive end, rather than by simple condemnation. For tragedy to be cogent in its own way, there must be pleasure in the destructiveness, pulls of some sort toward it; the cogency of merely moral control has been set aside by the heroic appeal to the expansive, poetic prospect of omnipotence. Ultimately the control in tragedy is death; the drama realizes the attraction of death, in one way for the protagonist, in another way for the audience." By creating *Doctor Faustus*, using tragic form "to cope with the blasphemous, heroic needs to which *Tamburlaine* had catered," Marlowe "finds and expresses a self-destructive motive concomitant to the characteristic Marlovian self-exaltation. The final death scene, integral with the rest of the play in imagery and motive, fulfills part of Faustus in destroying him. Meanwhile the author, in alliance with his audience, is well rid of his hero—for the time being, at least."

In Barber's understanding of the tragic irony of *Doctor Faustus*, the excruciating culmination of the play in Faustus's destruction is itself an expression of the protagonist's desire and of the need Marlowe brought to the creation of the play. To get at this dimension Barber put to use another development of Freudian thought. The illusion of psychic omnipotence, we have seen, can serve as an imaginary refuge from the constraints of social existence. But an extension of this presumption, its force turned back against the self, is manifest in the action of the psychic agency Freud called the superego. "The recognition that part of conscience is unconscious, and that it can be cruel, indeed, profoundly destructive, led Freud to introduce the construct of the superego. Difficult as this concept is, it seems to me very helpful in understanding Marlowe's need for blasphemy and for a medium through which it could be expressed and controlled."

Barber found the idea of the superego "difficult" in part because it could too easily lend itself to accounts that "trivialize, by psychologizing, so much that is beyond psychology—all those things in culture (and reality) which give conscience a social and more than social validity." But the danger thus posed is a reflection of what gives the concept its interpretive power, for it "is through the conception of a self-judging agency in the mind, largely unconscious, and shaped by the internalization of people taken as ideals, and through them of cultural ideals, that Freud made a bridge across from his individual psychology to culture and religion." Even when Freud's "ideas about culture and religion" are not adequate, Barber wrote, "one can still use the bridge"—in part because Freud's presentation of these ideas so consistently opens out to ranges of significance that he did not see or choose to explore. In following the logic of the superego in his own reading of Marlowe, Barber could rely extensively on Freud's summary statement of the concept in *The New Introductory Lectures on Psychoanalysis,* because there Freud "gives us, as always but exceptionally vividly, not just his ideas, but the motions of his mind in arriving at them, together with a lively sense that the subject is larger than his conclusions."

Freud's introduction of a new topography of the mind that included the superego "went with his increasing preoccupation with identification as a fundamental, shaping need" for the individual. "In his paper on 'Mourning and Melancholia,'[21] written in 1915, he developed the idea that the love of a person can be converted into an identification," preserving the other by making him or her into a part of the ego. In melancholia, Freud found, the process of preserving another by identification was complicated by feelings the sufferer may have never been aware of in his relationship to that person: "the cruel self-reproaches of the patients proved to be chiefly applicable not to themselves but to someone they have lost, and toward whom they entertained markedly ambivalent feelings. The superego, in this conception, is punishing the lost one, now become part of the ego." In another direction, Freud's preoccupation with the savagery of the superego and its explosive relation to social forms of violence reflected the massive brutality of the Great War and its aftermath: "The terrible facts of human aggression, destructiveness, and cruelty were urgently present to Freud during and after the war, and the tendency of his earlier work to see these chiefly as concomitants and aberrations of sexual needs gives way to the postulation of a primary destructive drive, the Thana-

21. See *Standard Edition,* 14:243–58.

tos of *Beyond the Pleasure Principle* (1920), now set up as the fundamental antagonist of Eros. Whatever one's attitude towards the speculation about ultimates in that essay (which has not been accepted by most of the professional psychoanalytic community), the other brilliant papers of the period provide illumination of the dark logic of destructiveness, particularly of the pattern of identification with a cruel superego which one can see in *Tamburlaine* and, with a difference, in *Doctor Faustus*.

By emphasizing the cruelty of the superego in reckoning with the brutality at work in Marlowe's art, Barber focused on a departure from what Freud understood as the "ideal" resolution of infantile conflict, in which the repression of forbidden desires is accompanied by the child's initial internalization of the parents' social values and, through this process of identification, new access to a more mature self-esteem. "In Freud's account of normal development, the transformation of an infant's love for his parents into identification with them goes with detaching libido from them and reinvesting it in the superego, and in the ego as narcissism. Such narcissism is not perverse (the single name for both is unfortunate); it is the self-love from which love buds out to lose part of the self in others, and it is a source of strength in the ego." Instead of developing as an agency that, along with the strictures it imposes, can provide an internalized continuation of parental love, the "cruel superego" is formed primarily on the basis of "the child's own desperate aggressive impulses." This aggression, fused with the erotic impulses that undergo repression, is turned back upon the self in order to avert the retaliation the child fears as a consequence of its direct expression. "The cruel superego, insofar as it is formed in this way by the recoil of the child's own aggressiveness, is not shaped by the transformation of love for the parent into identification. The parent has not been reached; the aggression is shaped in the awful isolation of helpless rage. Here I am glossing Freud with Faustus in mind (and, I must confess, also with thoughts of the horrors of aggression which have gone with the breakdown of tradition in our modern world). For the problem we find dramatized in *Doctor Faustus* is what to do without the love of God, or, more generalized, what to do if authority and force cannot go with love. In the benign development of the superego, which is motivated by Eros, authority and love do go

turned to the ego," and he adds, "perhaps it is only when the megalomania fails that the damming up of libido in the ego becomes pathogenic and starts the process of recovery which gives us the impression of a disease" (14:86). The pathogenic pattern here sketched is suggestively parallel to the movement in Marlowe's artistic development from Tamburlaine's celebration of his own glory to the desperate, tragic isolation of Faustus, who, his self-aggrandizing effort having proved self-destructive, is unable either to love the god he must acknowledge or to feel himself worthy of being loved by that god; the experience of being carried off to hell would parallel the pathogenic "attempt at restoration" of relationship through delusions of persecution.

The point, of course, is not that Marlowe's artistic development can be reduced to personal pathology, or that he could have made his life simpler, his art more benign, by embracing orthodox pieties that in both his life and work he calls into question. Marlowe's blasphemy in a religiously structured but volatile culture provided a way to a precarious liberation. In the new art form that made possible such expression, Marlowe sought theatrical equivalents for orthodox encounters with the divine. In the heroic drama of *Tamburlaine*, Marlowe found release from a particularly cruel superego—itself shaped by familial experience grounded in the orthodoxies of the culture—by creating a cruel figure of authority; instead of suffering cruelty, the threatened ego participates in the strong ideal figure's cruelty to others. The tragic movement of *Doctor Faustus* dramatizes both the failure of love bypassed in *Tamburlaine* and the inescapability for its protagonist of encounter with, even desire for, a cruelly vindictive deity.

With Tamburlaine, whose exploits are analogous to what Freud described as the manic absorption of the superego into egoistic interest, aggressive and erotic energies are fused in destruction directed out against a social world. "The tendency to self-destruction is kept entirely below the surface by the efficiency of his aggression, the constant putting out, onto others, of obsessive images of agony and death. But even in Tamburlaine, . . . the aggressive instinct is complicated by Eros." With Faustus, for whom the cruelty of the superego is, as in melancholia, turned back upon himself, the destructive impulse carries with it the force of Eros; the play expresses as a self-destructive motive the hero's need to be loved. "Doing without love, in Freud's psychology, is strictly speaking impossible. Thus in melancholia, 'the ego gives itself up because it feels itself hated and persecuted by the superego, instead of being loved' (*The Ego and the Id,* p. 58)." But this hatred includes within itself the erotic component denied more direct expression for the melancholiac, either as the narcissistic love that sustains the ego or as the love of an object in the world. The ego's surrender is a yielding to a self-destructive force fused with Eros. "And so, when we come to look at the final scene of *Doctor Faustus,* we shall have a basis for understanding the sexualization of the expected death by associations relating it to an assault by Lucifer. If, as Freud argues in *The Ego and the Id,* behind the fear of death is the fear of castration, grounded in the formative period of the superego, then an acceptance of castration, of the negative oedipal relation which takes a feminine attitude toward the father, would mitigate the final horror of encountering Thanatos. In more general terms, the sexualization of death in tragedy is of course very widespread: fusion of love with death serves to make the idea of death endurable."

Here the logic of Faustus's self-destructive quest again points to the complex relation of tragedy and religion, for love and death are, of course, also fused in Christ's crucifixion, which makes death endurable for his worshipers through the promise of everlasting life. Christ's voluntary sacrifice, his death as a man in loving acquiescence to his father's will, is the mark of his divinity. What the Communion offers the worshiper, access to deity through Christ's sacrifice, tragedy dramatizes as impossible at the level of individual aspiration—but through an action that confirms the precarious, heroic authenticity of this impossible aspiration. "In watching a tragedy, we participate vicariously in an involuntary sacrifice. What is sacrificed is a potential divinity in man, and we feel the reality of this, with the effect of an epiphany showing forth of the god. We experience a qualm of awe and a sense of tragic loss and also a reassuring return of control at the end."

The kind of control achieved by tragic form works very differently from that of religious ritual in the church. "The church, a place apart of long standing, was 'holy' in the full sense, hedged about with sanctions to control the motives expressed within it. But the theater, once it was endowed with such power of expression as Marlowe brought to it, offered an opportunity for enactment whose limits were not yet known." To observe Marlowe achieving tragic form in *Doctor Faustus* is to see the theater coming into "its proper relation to the whole society as a resource for exploring and understanding human possibilities and limits."

"The relation of liturgy to the worshipers is of course different from that of drama to author or audience. For the worshipers, what happens in worship *is* an event"—an event that takes place inside the symbolic order of the culture and that directly enacts the worshipers' place within that order. "What happens in drama is distinguished from events; we now habitually speak of imitation or expression" and thus implicitly recognize the remove from actual living that the theater provides. "But we too often forget that the aesthetic distance of drama, its status as art, is a relationship which has to be established and maintained. When a new art form is being created, its status as art is not self-evident and must be worked out. Thus the Tudor drama of the formative period is preoccupied with inductions, presenters, framing stories, all serving to mark off art from life. More fundamental in achieving the status of art for the drama is the control of identification with its protagonists and poetry, the development of dramatic irony, and through poetry and irony, the balance of the whole form." It is this "crucial balance," not yet attained in *Tamburlaine* and *The Spanish Tragedy*, that is "fully achieved for the first time in tragedy in *Doctor Faustus*."

The achievement of this kind of distance in the drama answered a need for it generated by far-reaching changes in European culture as its tradition-directed society, dominated by ceremony and ritual, gave way to a society that came to know itself and its members through historical and psychological awareness. In approaching this transition, Barber wrote, "our difficulty is to imagine the first view, for our assumptions are shaped by the second to the point where its perspectives seem inevitable." If we proceed to make a "psychological analysis," we tend to "look to the individuals involved and their motives, as though the individuals existed separately from and prior to their situation." If, on the other hand, we produce a "historical analysis," we tend to "look to the situation involved and its history, as though the situation existed separately from or prior to the individuals." The "pluralistic, eclectic, rapidly changing culture" we live in makes "this way of thinking 'natural.' It is hard for us to realize that in a unified, traditional, relatively static culture, individuals are not regularly separated out from their situations."

It would be "nostalgic sentimentality" to assume of such a society, that "because cultural forms were inevitable, they were satisfactory." And "there is, of course, no society where individuals are totally merged with cultural forms—anthropologists find the most culture-bound people to be individuals and to be preoccupied with individual ambitions, individual differentiations. But the more traditional cultures do not have our ways of focusing on the psychological and the historical because their modes of symbolic action are given, accepted, *engaging*, as a matter of course." In such a culture, in short, there is no place for an art that does what the art of Marlowe or Kyd or Shakespeare does with the freedom of a new disengagement by dramatic form. Barber saw the achievement of Renaissance drama "as a way of breaking free (or partly free) from the identification of the individual and his situation" basic to traditional cultures.

The enormously complex and varied developments in the emergence of early modern Europe from its late medieval roots will not, of course, fit neatly into the "clear-cut antitheses" of ideal types of culture—traditional and modern. "Between monolithic cultures, where symbolic action, traditionally prescribed, largely submerges individual constructions, and loose-structured, eclectic modern cosmopolitan society, there are clearly many intermediate situations, variations by epochs and regions, and by social groups within them. . . . Elizabethan England," Barber observed, "is a complex case in point":

> The church was a locale where the society agreed that ritual action should be rigidly prescribed; yet within the church, ritual was under the strains of the Reformation, involving conflicts about the form and meaning of the liturgy, notably the Communion and the nature of the elements of bread and wine. Profound aggressions were developed about these issues. Outside the church, too,

there were rituals of state which functioned to contain, often precariously, strong disruptive tendencies. It was in this unstable institutional situation that the theater was emerging. Into the theater came Marlowe, whose disruptive personal disposition we cannot possibly doubt: we overhear his aggression against society in the reports of his scorner's talk about religion—the Virgin a whore, John, Christ's Ganymede; his right to coin money as good as the Queen's; those who use not boys and tobacco are fools, etc.

Without the drama, the need in Marlowe that could lead to such aggression "would have remained beneath the surface of culture, erupting in such merely personal assertion and violence as we glimpse in a court record and in the testimony of Kyd and Baines." "The fascinating thing is that when this aggression is brought into the theater, the social necessities of art transform it into a social action—tragedy. . . . When enacted in the theater, the motives become something held in common social perspective. . . . Drama and ritual are not the same thing"— but the drama addresses itself to needs in a society that in other circumstances fall within the domain of ritual confirmation of shared social awareness.

"The whole process of creation is a dynamic encounter of author with audience which cannot be reduced to 'a psychology.'" Marlowe used the drama "for the assertion and defense of an ego which, as I think his works will testify, was constantly threatened by powerful forces of desire and conscience, forces which he coped with as best he could by making them conscious, by finding a form for them which would command social understanding and the control of shared social attitudes." We can look through his plays to "see, if only darkly, into Marlowe's motives for creating them, understanding something of his need to create such drama." But in doing so we are also engaged in "understanding something of the Reformation-Renaissance crisis in which this need took shape. In the process we can see Marlowe finding his way to the logic of dramatic form, as dramatic form functions to establish and maintain the difference between art and life."

It was in the creation of this difference, Barber believed, that Elizabethan drama could make a difference in the way people perceived their social and individual lives. "The great dramatists had to win their way to a dramatic view of man that we take for granted, and the great drama *is* the process of this winning. Once the dramatic view had been fully established, the drama declined because it had no longer any function as a way of exploring and changing society." In its great moment, however, the Elizabethan drama provided "a new way of framing and testing experience. The new drama was not simply an expression of change; during the brief period of its vitality, it was an agency, a means of making the Renaissance shift from a ceremonial and ritualistic view of life toward a psychological and historical view." The chapters of this book present Barber's understanding of the contributions Marlowe and Kyd made to their historical moment and its way of registering an experience of change and dislocation that remains a part of our unstable cultural inheritance.

I

Theatrical Magic
in *Tamburlaine*

I hold the Fates bound fast in yron chaines,
And with my hand turne Fortunes wheel about.

A *Novum Organum*

The sudden emergence of the Elizabethan drama was a step in
the developing self-consciousness of modern culture; it provided a new way of envisaging and testing experience which remains fundamental for us, so that we continue to be occupied
with what happened in that moment. What was involved in
the creation of Elizabethan tragedy is especially visible in Marlowe's astonishing work, coming at the very beginning of the
great, brief period and contributing so much to later writers,
particularly Shakespeare. In his *Tamburlaine* and *Doctor Faustus,* and in Kyd's great *Spanish Tragedy* of the same formative
moment, we can see the theater becoming a new organ of culture, in tension with older, more established forms of expression. These pioneering masterpieces, where potentialities of the
new medium suddenly emerged, make clear much about the
medium itself, and about the theater as a social institution—an
agency of change as well as an expression of it. So in addition to

their great intrinsic interest, these plays can provide perspective on Shakespeare's use of this new theatrical situation, his
ways of finding himself in it. That Marlowe's self-asserting,
domineering sensibility is almost a polar opposite to Shakespeare's, while Kyd's is in some ways kindred, contributes to this
interest.

To look first at *Tamburlaine* and then at *Doctor Faustus* will
also permit us to pursue relationships between the Reformation
and the new drama. The fact that Reformation and Renaissance happen simultaneously in England is nowhere clearer than
in these two plays. The creation of the new art form put men in
a new relationship to their experience, in some ways analogous
to the relationship to reality developed by the reformers. This is
the clearer in the Marlowe plays because they reflect, in displaced ways in *Tamburlaine* and directly in *Doctor Faustus*, the
"Puritan" or Calvinist strain of the Reformation, by contrast
with what one can call—again with displacement—Shakespeare's Anglican sensibility.

The repertory theater constituted a new place apart, alternative to the church, where human possibilities could be envisaged with a new freedom. Marlowe seems perfectly conscious
that he is making the theater a new organ of consciousness:

> Onely this (Gentlemen) we must performe,
> The form of *Faustus* fortunes good or bad.
> To patient Iudgements we appeale our plaude.
>
> (*Faus.*, 7–9)[1]

From the critical distance of the audience watching impas-
sioned claims on meaning with "patient Iudgements," there was
the potentiality of awareness similar to that which led Luther
and subsequent reformers to dismiss "works" as useless for salvation because they were only the doings of men, not God. Such
critical perspective in the religious development proved difficult
indeed to stop, both in individual anguish about election and in
the proliferation of competing sects. As Stephen Greenblatt

---

1. C. F. Tucker Brooke's edition of *The Works of Christopher Marlowe*
numbers the lines consecutively through each play and through the two parts
of *Tamburlaine*.

observes in his superb study *Renaissance Self-Fashioning*, illustrating the process movingly with More and Tyndale, "Protestant and Catholic polemicists demonstrated brilliantly how each other's religion—the very anchor of reality for millions of souls—was a cunning theatrical illusion, a demonic fantasy, a piece of poetry. Each conducted this unmasking, of course, in the name of the *real* religious truth." [2]

Equivalents of individualistic "prophesying," in secular versions, were of course crucial in the drama. The leaders of the reformed churches had such difficulty controlling "the liberty of prophesying" because it expressed, in popular, often antinomian ways, the new sense of individuality validated by unmediated relation to deity which they themselves brought to Europe. Poetry of magical expectation, linked to dramatic action so as to put pressure on it and be contradicted by it, is absolutely crucial in animating the major drama's exploration of human possibility and so its new visions of the human situation. It is cognate with the sense of new possibilities in the whole age, which included, along with new forms of religious individuality, the substratum of folk magic and the learned aspirations for magical dominion of the Hermetic and kindred philosophies. The ambiguous relations of magical possibilities with religion, with the cult of royal powers, and again, with incipient natural science, are made sources of dramatic energy and stress.

To look at the achieved balance of the masterpieces of Elizabethan tragedy can obscure what was involved in bringing under control the disruptive potential of this poetic theater. The magical release of poetry in alliance with mimetic action opened possibilities for aggression by the dramatist in the service of his own drives toward omnipotence of mind. To understand the development of tragic form, the need for it, we need to recover the profoundly disruptive potentiality of this imaginative freedom at the moment when the new art form was nascent. Because we take the freedom of the theater for granted, we can easily overlook the Elizabethan problem of controlling it—controlling its freedom not merely as an external threat to social order but as a threat to the internal order of the psyche.

---

2. *Renaissance Self-Fashioning: From More to Shakespeare* (Chicago: University of Chicago Press, 1980), p. 219.

Before the new Renaissance drama, the Christian cycle plays and the moralities were congruent with the society's cosmology, eschatology, and morality. Disruptive trends of folk plays and festivities were contained by the saturnalian rhythm which licensed inversions and release from social awe only in holiday moments or special occasions within the cycle of the year. After the brief, vital moment of Elizabethan dramatic development, some thirty or forty years, the theatrical had become a familiar amusement and the theater a cyst within the social organism. But in the vital years of the new drama, theatrical magic could have a threatening, outrageous power, especially so at the outset. Marlowe's *Tamburlaine* and, in its different way, Kyd's *Spanish Tragedy* are disruptive plays where theatrical aggression goes out of control.

We can see the process of bringing theatrical magic under the control of tragic form by looking first at *Tamburlaine* and then at *Doctor Faustus*. Exploration of the relationships between the two works has convinced me that Marlowe's great tragedy comes soon after the heroic drama of conquest and not, as some suppose, at the close of Marlowe's development.[3] The two parts of *Tamburlaine* and *Doctor Faustus* contain most of

---

3. In his 1910 edition of Marlowe, Brooke placed *Doctor Faustus* next after *Tamburlaine* but subsequently argued for a later date in "The Marlowe Canon," *PMLA* 37 (1922): 379–84. W. W. Greg decided for a date of 1592 or later in his edition, *Marlowe's "Doctor Faustus," 1604–1616: Parallel Texts* (Oxford: Clarendon Press, 1950), p. 10. If, as Greg argues, Marlowe's source, the English Faust-book, first appeared close to the 1592 court case over its publication rights, a later date would seem necessary. But Harold Jenkins has observed, in a review of Greg's edition (*Modern Language Review* 46 [1951]: 86), that "there is stronger evidence for dating [the Faust-book] not later than 1590 than for dating it not earlier than 1592." For arguments that place *Doctor Faustus* as the successor to *Tamburlaine* see M. M. Mahood's chapter "Marlowe's Heroes" in *Poetry and Humanism* (London: Jonathon Cape, 1950) and J. B. Steane's chapter on *Doctor Faustus* in *Marlowe: A Critical Study* (Cambridge: Cambridge University Press, 1964), especially pp. 117–19. Steane cites Jenkins's challenge of Greg, but the chief basis of his argument for an earlier date, like Mahood's, rests on "affinities of style and thought" (p. 119) between *Tamburlaine* and *Doctor Faustus* and on an overall pattern in the main line of Marlowe's development from the expansiveness of *Tamburlaine* through the dramatization of an increasingly constricted range of human possibility in *Doctor Faustus, The Jew Of Malta,* and *Edward II* (see p. 347).

Marlowe's high-flaming poetry, for that poetry is characteristically his vehicle for experience galvanized by expectations of omnipotence, or admiration of the aura of it. These plays are distinguished among Marlowe's works by their preoccupation with omnipotence and with worship. Except at anguished moments in *Doctor Faustus*, it is not properly religious worship, but what would be religious were it not that the worship is directed at other than divine objects, the divine diffused and displaced. In *Tamburlaine*, the principal object of enthralled worship is the hero, except where Tamburlaine in his turn worships Zenocrate. In *Doctor Faustus*, a dependent relationship like that between the author of *Tamburlaine* and its hero is put *inside* the play, as the pact between the magus and Mephostophilis. *Tamburlaine* is a strange, anomalous work because it embodies the release of energy characteristic of Elizabethan tragedy, but in a heroic form which puzzles our sensibilities, conditioned as they are by the tragedies which followed. It is both highly intelligent and deeply naive, drama written partly in defiance and partly in ignorance of the limits of art. It overrides potential ironies, miming omnipotence by confirming, in stage action, magical expectations launched by Marlowe's "mighty line." Then in *Doctor Faustus*, in the hero's effort to achieve omnipotence through actual magic, Marlowe conducts what amounts to an experiment to test such possibilities—"thinke so still, till experience change thy minde" (560).

Marlowe's rapid, direct route to tragedy provides a revealing contrast to Shakespeare's far more complex development, which does not come to concentrate on tragedy until his poems and more than half of his plays had been written. The contrast is the more revealing because Marlowe in his brief career, cut short by a moment in life when the violence which preoccupies his art turned a dagger to his head, commanded properly artistic powers almost equal to Shakespeare's. He had a greater range of scholarly learning, and equal or perhaps greater *executive* intelligence, though not equal intelligence of still more important kinds. The greatness of the very greatest artists depends on the human resources they bring to their art as well as on their genius for artistic innovation. Marlowe's humanity limits his art at the same time that it motivates his breakthroughs.

Doctor Faustus, as a commentary on *Tamburlaine*, dramatizes the limitations with a marvelous clarity and cogency, at once appalling and awesome as an achievement of tragic recognition. In looking at how and why Marlowe made a new dramatic form, I shall restrict my concern to these two moments in his rapid and always innovative development, leaving to the side, for the most part, the poems, the beautiful, dramatically imaginative adaptation of Virgil in *Dido, Queen of Carthage* and the compacted, rigorously theatrical explorations of power and desire which, in my view of the process of his growth, follow the high poetry of *Tamburlaine* and *Doctor Faustus*. My concern is to consider *Faustus* as a reckoning with and mastery of much that is not faced in *Tamburlaine*. It is always possible, of course, that the close relationship of these two plays reflects the deep continuity—the permanence, so to speak—in a great artist of his deepest concerns, and that one was written at the beginning of Marlowe's brief career, the other near the end. But in the absence of compelling external evidence, it seems logical that *The Jew of Malta* and *Edward II*—two plays which make comedy and tragedy of human life lived entirely without grace—should be regarded as following the plays which present Tamburlaine taking grace by assault and then Faustus trying and failing to find a substitute for grace in diabolical magic. The harsh intellectual farce of *The Jew of Malta* and the tragic realism of *Edward II* are stunning achievements in their own kinds, the latter play a tragic reckoning with motives central to *Doctor Faustus*. But, for the purposes of this study, I do not think it necessary to consider Marlowe's whole oeuvre to gain an understanding of the temperament which animates it.

In creating, with *Doctor Faustus*, the first fully achieved Elizabethan tragedy, Marlowe controls, by means of the theater, creative and destructive energies released by the theater. At the moment of most intense crisis in Shakespeare's development, we get a failure of such control—in *Hamlet*. The result is a marvelous work of perennial, open-ended significance, because the energies set loose in *Hamlet* by the encounter on the battlements license a relationship of the protagonist to his world that proves to be beyond full understanding within the play. Shakespeare's need for relationship to an ideal father, emerging from shiftings in the structuring motives of his work, leads to his exploiting the disruptive potentialities of the theater to present, in the ghost, a psychological projection as real. In *Othello*, we can see his turning around on *Hamlet* to achieve tragic recognition and control of motives incompletely mastered in the earlier play, somewhat as Marlowe turns around on *Tamburlaine* in *Doctor Faustus*.[4]

Theatrical Omnipotence

If we call the things Marlowe presents in the two parts of *Tamburlaine* by their moral names, he was not treating anything new: there was nothing new about blasphemous defiance, tyranny, self-idolatry, cruelty. What was new was that *Tamburlaine* presents these things, programmatically and unqualifiedly, as heroic achievement. There is no stable moral, eschatological framework, such as we get in *De Casibus* literature like *The Mirror for Magistrates*. There is no peripeteia: Tamburlaine's death is presented simply as the result of the exhaustion of his natural vital powers as he looks beyond it for further similar conquests by his sons. The two parts are so radically and consistently amoral or antimoral that they are hard to read in their own terms, as the record of criticism shows. Most readers cannot resist bringing in their own moral response and moral terms; they record their own gradual alienation from the hero despite the poetry's unflagging exaltations of him. Or at the furthest extreme, Roy Battenhouse mobilizes theological and political considerations from the period about the role of the Scourge of God to make a consistent framework such as Marlowe himself does not provide, and concludes that the play is "one of the most grandly moral spectacles in the whole realm of English drama."[5]

---

4. See the discussion of *Othello* as a development from the situation in *Hamlet* in chap. 8 of C. L. Barber and Richard P. Wheeler, *The Whole Journey: Shakespeare's Power of Development* (Berkeley and Los Angeles: University of California Press, 1986), pp. 272–81.

5. *Marlowe's Tamburlaine: A Study in Renaissance Moral Philosophy* (Nashville, Tenn.: Vanderbilt University Press, 1941), p. 258. Battenhouse's extraordinary reading of the play is learnedly informative about theories of the Scourge of God and much else, an extremely useful book for historical background, but his interpretation asks us to substitute sympathy with moral cruelty for participation in amoral or antimoral heroic endeavor.

It is crucial not to lose touch, as so much criticism does in describing "content," with the process by which the play realizes itself as an experience. Moment by moment, poetry is so combined with action as to force us to participate in Tamburlaine's self-aggrandizement. We can, however, see into the underlying tensions at work in the process of creation of the play by looking at the moments when Tamburlaine encounters limitation. They center not on morality, which he consistently and zestfully overrides, nor on death, but in his worshipful relationship to Zenocrate. In marked contrast to Shakespeare, Marlowe is primarily concerned not with transmission of heritage across the generations but with the usurpation of heritage by a single hero in a single generation. But through Tamburlaine's relation to Zenocrate we can see how the sensibility which needed the play and its hero is shaped by a latent family constellation.

In considering the structural resources Marlowe developed for the new drama, the crucial thing is not only the power of his poetry but the way the poetry is used to put pressure on the stage action. Studies of many kinds since the beginning of this century have made us aware, as earlier scholars were not, of the essential contributions which the popular theater made to the great poetic drama which emerges so suddenly in the late 1580s. We now realize that the theater was very much a going concern before the university wits gave it their voice; it had accomplished actors, a responsive audience. Judging by the few surviving examples, its repertoire of plays had conventional roles and scenes of great dramatic potential whose structural contribution to the works of the great period we more and more appreciate. Yet the advent of real poetry was crucial, and, as T. S. Eliot insisted, it was not poetry as "an added embellishment" to drama, but poetry and dramatic action working together.[6] The earlier theater's double medium, of expression in words and expression in physical gesture, typically produced

---

6. "Poetry and Drama" (1951), in *On Poetry and Poets* (1957; reprint, New York: Noonday Press, 1961), p. 75. See also "A Dialogue on Dramatic Poetry" (1928), in *Selected Essays*, new ed. (New York: Harcourt, Brace and World, 1950), pp. 31–45, and "The Three Voices of Poetry" (1953), in *On Poetry and Poets*, pp. 96–112.

what M. C. Bradbrook has aptly summarized as pantomime accompanied by declamation.[7] Words and gestures in the surviving early plays typically run parallel, reduplicating each other: people on the stage say what the situation is, who they are, and what they are doing, their words flapping along beside their actions in the present indicative.

But the high poetry in *Tamburlaine* is not shaped to express what is but to make something happen, or, by a kind of incantation, to make something have happened. The verbs are commonly future or imperative, rather than present indicative: "For Wil and Shall best fitteth *Tamburlain*" (1139). When they state something in the present, it is something hyperbolic:

> I hold the Fates bound fast in yron chaines,
> And with my hand turne Fortunes wheel about,
>
> . . . .
>
> Draw foorth thy sword, thou mighty man at Armes,
> Intending but to rase my charmed skin:
> And *Ioue* himselfe will stretch his hand from heauen,
> To ward the blow, and shield me safe from harme.
>
> (369–70, 373–76)

Marlowe takes two of the most established symbols of human limitation, the Fates and Fortune's wheel, and lets his actor, the great Edward Alleyn, manhandle them in gesture. Jove's intervention is then confirmed by Tamburlaine's pointing to something physically present on the stage, the captured Egyptian treasure:

> See how he raines down heaps of gold in showers,
> As if he meant to giue my Souldiers pay.
>
> (377–78)

7. In *Themes and Conventions of Elizabethan Tragedy* (Cambridge: Cambridge University Press, 1935), Bradbrook notes that "plays seem to divide into passages of declaimed speech, and passages of action of a violent and conventional kind" (p. 27), but observes the importance of refinements that increasingly brought the poetry into the service of action: "The blank verse was not at first a speech cadence, though later writers used a more colloquial movement, and presumably the enunciation changed in consequence. Perhaps the modification of blank verse was the most important controlling factor of the delivery" (p. 24).

This sort of confirmation of the imagined in the physical appears also, of course, in the larger dramatic movement. Marlowe's prologue summarizes the sequence:

> *From iygging vaines of riming mother wits,*
>
> . . . .
> *Weele lead you to the stately tent of War,*
> *Where you shall heare the Scythian Tamburlaine*
> *Threatning the world with high astounding tearms*
> *And scourging kingdoms with his conquering sword.*
>
> (1, 3–6)

The verse is always rooted in a stage situation, even when it moves up and out in its highest reaches. A telling example is the famous generalizing passage of self-justification after Tamburlaine has defeated Cosroe, the Persian prince whom he had helped gain his brother's throne. In answer to Cosroe's demanding his reason for his treachery, Tamburlaine's language soars out over the writhing body:

> The thirst of raigne and sweetnes of a crown,
> That causde the eldest sonne of heauenly *Ops*,
> To thrust his doting father from his chaire,
> And place himselfe in the Emperiall heauen,
> Moou'd me to manage armes against thy state.
> What better president than mightie *Ioue?*
> Nature that fram'd vs of foure Elements,
> Warring within our breasts for regiment,
> Doth teach vs all to haue aspyring minds:
> Our soules, whose faculties can comprehend
> The wondrous Architecture of the world:
> And measure euery wandring plannets course,
> Still climing after knowledge infinite,
> And alwaies moouing as the restles Spheares,
> Wils vs to weare our selues and neuer rest,
> Vntill we reach the ripest fruit of all,
> That perfect blisse and sole felicitie,
> The sweet fruition of an earthly crowne.
>
> (863–80)

The frequent complaint that the last line is a letdown neglects the fact that on stage the crown is right there, on dying Cosroe's head, so that after his final death agony Tamburlaine can put it on his own head with "Who thinke you now is king of *Persea?*" (907). Marlowe is as avid for actuality as he is for mythic and scientific vision. The radical redefinition of the humors as not normally in equilibrium but in constant war is peculiarly Marlovian, together with simultaneous relish for freedom and mastery in "measure euery wandring plannets course." The passage reflects his participation in the new intellectual developments of the age, its opening universe. To feel "the sweet fruition of an earthly crown" as an anticlimax is to sentimentalize the age, as Stephen Greenblatt makes toughly clear in his splendid study of Marlowe's participation in and understanding of the ruthless appropriation of that opening world: [8]

> Men from the farthest Equinoctiall line,
> Haue swarm'd in troopes into the Easterne India:
> Lading their shippes with golde and pretious stones.
>
> (127–29)

The appropriation of names and ceremonies is integral to the aggrandizing process. The theatrical situation had always, by necessary convention, allowed for characters to name themselves. Marlowe uses the convention in a new way: Tamburlaine—and hero after hero after him—talks continually about himself as though from outside, using his own name in an incantatory fashion which amplifies his identity. He can create himself out of nothing, an emperor out of a shepherd, by redefining his name by reference to things on stage. When Zenocrate addresses him as "my Lord," he answers, "I am a Lord, for so my deeds shall prooue" (229–30), and proceeds to confirm this new title by action, taking off his shepherd's clothes and putting on armor he has just captured:

8. See "Marlowe and the Will to Absolute Play," chap. five in *Renaissance Self-Fashioning.* At the center of the "historical matrix of Marlowe's achievement," Greenblatt puts "the acquisitive energies of English merchants, entrepreneurs, and adventurers, promoters alike of trading companies and theatrical companies" (p. 194). "Marlowe writes in the period in which European man embarked on his extraordinary career of consumption, his eager pursuit of knowledge, with one intellectual model after another seized, squeezed dry, and discarded, and his frenzied exhaustion of the world's resources" (p. 199).

Lie here ye weedes that I disdaine to weare,
This compleat armor, and this curtle-axe
Are adiuncts more beseeming *Tamburlaine.*

(237–39)

Tamburlaine is a play of ceremonies and processions: crowning Cosroe, crowning Tamburlaine, uncrowning the Turkish
empress to place her crown on Zenocrate's head, Tamburlaine
mounting his throne on Bajazeth as a footstool, Tamburlaine in
his chariot drawn by captive kings. This delight in pomp is
characteristic of the popular theater both before and after the
emergence of major drama; Robert Wilson's jingoistic *Three
Lords and Ladies of London,* for example, makes up for lame language by parading about the stage London's Pomp, London's
Treasure, and so on. Such theatrical pageantry was the stage's
equivalent for the actual Elizabethan progresses, ceremonial
tournaments, and processions of the court and civic bodies, and
also for the processional pageantry of narrative poetry, as in
Spenser's *Faerie Queene.* The governing idea of such pagentry,
akin to the establishing of spiritual relations in ecclesiastical rituals, was that the procession unrolls persons or allegorical figures in their due and proper order, with their right names and in
their right places. Marlowe's Tamburlaine is a great ritualist, but
he designs his own ceremonies, and they are all, like the first
one of arming himself, aimed at aggrandizing his identity, indeed, creating it. He sets them up because "This is my minde,
and I will haue it so" (1535). Once set up, he maintains them
as though they had the inevitability of sanctified custom—as
with the sequence of his white, red, and black costume and
tents on successive days of a siege.

To take over ceremonies can be a way of taking over social
identity. As he takes over, Tamburlaine delights in demonstrat-
ing that words and things, titles and persons, do not necessarily
go together for *others.* A justly famous moment comes after Cosroe, with Tamburlaine's help, has defeated Mycetes:

Cosroe: Farewell Lord Regent, and his happie friends,
         I long to sit vpon my brothers throne.
Meander: Your Maiestie shall shortly haue your wish,
          And ride in triumph through *Persepolis.*   *Exeunt.*

Manent Tamburlaine, Techelles, Theridamas, Vsumcasane.
TAMBURLAINE: And ride in triumph through *Persepolis?*
    Is it not braue to be a King, *Techelles?*
    Vsumcasane and *Theridamas,*
    Is it not passing braue to be a King,
    And ride in triumph through *Persepolis?*
TECHELLES: O my Lord, tis sweet and full of pompe.
VSUMCASANE: To be a King, is halfe to be a God.
THERIDAMAS: A God is not so glorious as a King:
    I thinke the pleasure they enioy in heauen
    Can not compare with kingly ioyes in earth.
    To weare a Crowne enchac'd with pearle and golde,
    Whose vertues carie with it life and death,
    To aske, and haue: commaund, and be obeied:
    When looks breed loue, with lookes to gaine the prize.
    Such power attractiue shines in princes eies.

                                  (751–69)

Tamburlaine reaches up as the grand phrase about triumph hangs in the air, seizes it, and tries it on for size. It is ironic, *for Cosroe,* that kingship is not an absolute; for Tamburlaine it means a special kind of aggressive pleasure, consummated when, after Cosroe's defeat, he crowns himself.

But this involves, we notice, a curious paradox: he has the cake of kingship and eats it too. As his followers describe it, to be a king is "To aske, and haue: commaund, and be obeied," to be without human limitations. Marlowe in *Tamburlaine* is constantly having it both ways like this, relishing the failure of absolutes for conquered monarchs while celebrating his hero's absolute faith in his own fated greatness. Tamburlaine has just made fun of the physical symbol Theridamas is in awe of, in the scene where Mycetes is planning to hide his crown. The ninny king explains his purpose in the "iygging vaines" of the "riming mother wits":

                    a goodly Stratagem,
    And far from any man that is a foole.
    So shall not I be knowen, or if I bee,
    They cannot take away my crowne from me.
    Here will I hide it in this simple hole.

                              (674–78)

When the Turkish empress's crown is wrenched from her head and placed on Zenocrate's ("Howe dare you thus abuse my Maiesty?"), Tamburlaine explains with ruthless clarity: "The pillers that haue bolstered vp those tearmes / Are falne in clusters at my conquering feet" (1324, 1327–28). In a later scene, there is the banquet of crowns. After Bajazeth, starving in his cage, has been mocked and forced to eat table scraps, crowns are served up for the victors: "*Enter a second course of Crownes.*" Tamburlaine sets about crowning his followers with "*Theridamas, Techelles* and *Casane,* here are the cates you desire to finger, are they not?" (1747–48).

There is a magnificent, brutal mastery in calling crowns "cates" and in speaking of the followers' desire to "finger" them—they would not dare eat them, as Tamburlaine does, but by his leave. He almost scorns the world's absolutes because, in subduing them, he shows them not to be absolutes after all. He moves *through* geography, cosmology, royalty, but there is nowhere for him to arrive; he is essentially a disruptive energy, to be defined only dynamically, that is, dramatically.

The whole process would not work if crowns did not remain crowns, gods gods, however much the hero manhandles them. Marlowe was writing at the beginning of what C. S. Lewis called the golden moment of Renaissance poetry, when value seemed to be naturally in the world, out there, waiting to be put into words—or there in words, waiting to be put into poetry.[9] The values of the received cosmos, what Lewis described so well in *The Discarded Image,*[10] are built into *la langue,* flowering indeed with a special vividness as new freedom of *parole* disrupts them. Marlowe uses the hierarchies as the ladder of a high design even while negating the attitudes of reverence that sustained them. The whole Elizabethan drama, indeed, depends on this paradoxical relation of objective value and subjective freedom. When the value out there had been used up by the liberties taken with it, the great moment of the drama was over.

9. See *English Literature in the Sixteenth Century, Excluding Drama* (London: Oxford University Press, 1954), pp. 64–65 and Book 2, passim.
10. Cambridge: Cambridge University Press, 1964.

"I know not how to take their tyrannies"

The criticism of *Tamburlaine* could take the line I quote above—spoken by the dying Cosroe after Tamburlaine's "thirst of raigne" self-justification—as a motto. In part our perplexity about "the strangest men that euer nature made" (891) is owing to Marlowe's failure to articulate fully the significance of his hero. But his hero's undefinable quality is built into the dramatic movement, as we have seen, and crucial for his function for the author and audience. That he is beyond definition is explicitly dramatized in the response of Cosroe's followers after Tamburlaine turns on them. Cosroe is enough of a Marlowe-style king to put himself in Jove's place and ask how Tamburlaine can dare, titanlike, to threaten the frame of things:

> What means this diuelish shepheard to aspire
> With such a Giantly presumption,
> To cast vp hils against the face of heuen:
> And dare the force of angrie *Iupiter*.
>
> (812–15)

But Cosroe's followers, in trying to place Tamburlaine, demonstrate that established categories will not work:

> MEANDER: Some powers diuine, or els infernall, mixt
>   Their angry seeds at his conception:
>   For he was neuer sprong of humaine race,
>   Since with the spirit of his fearefull pride,
>   He dares so doubtlesly resolue of rule,
>   And by profession be ambitious.
> ORTYGIUS: What God or Feend, or spirit of the earth,
>   Or Monster turned to a manly shape,
>   Or of what mould or mettel he be made,
>   What star or state soeuer gouerne him,
>   Let vs put on our meet incountring mindes,
>   And in detesting such a diuelish Thiefe,
>   In loue of honor & defence of right,
>   Be arm'd against the hate of such a foe,
>   Whether from earth, or hell, or heuen he grow.
>
> (820–34)

Brought up on Shakespeare, we are apt to take as a matter of course this sort of triangulation by language on something beyond it, especially as Marlowe's coordinates, though wonderfully bold, are relatively simple. But an immense, desperate energy was required to initiate the use of dramatic form to break apart words and things so as to make way for indefinable energies. It is striking that we get a very similarly open-ended description when Hamlet first encounters the ghost:

> Angels and ministers of grace defend us!
> Be thou a spirit of health or goblin damn'd,
> Bring with thee airs from heaven, or blasts from hell,
> Be thy intents wicked or charitable,
> Thou com'st in such a questionable shape
> That I will speak to thee. I'll call thee Hamlet,
> King, father, royal Dane.
>
> (1.4.39–45)

Hamlet's "I'll call thee" wills a definition he is determined to make good. The sequel justifies him—all too well, as I see the play and its failure to provide a dramatic perspective from which the ghost's status can be adequately comprehended—though doubts recur: "The spirit that I have seen / May be a dev'l" (2.2.598–99). The ghastly bewilderment in Horatio's earlier "In what particular thought to work I know not" (1.1.67) remains part of the whole response, for characters in the play, for the audience—and for criticism, which has sought endlessly to contain the ghost's fundamentally ambiguous presence within a dramatically coherent frame of reference.

Seen from a Freudian vantage point, Shakespeare's play splits the figure of the father into the exalted ghost and the detestable, menacing Claudius. Through his filial identification with the exalted father, Hamlet gains a manic energy with which to confront a court and a world put out of joint by Claudius. Marlowe does not dramatize affiliation to Tamburlaine by identification, nor is Tamburlaine a father figure. Instead, he is an identity created to cope with father figures. The assumption of the play is that only a quasi-divine identity and energy can do this; the omnipotent father of infancy—or the divine father—is present, as occasions demand, as example or again as sanction, but he is present primarily as rival.

That Tamburlaine should be beyond limitation and so definition, and "alwaies moouing as the restles Spheares" (876), goes with a deep underlying anxiety that springs from the assumption that no atonement with paternal or royal or ultimate power is possible. That rebellion is the necessary proof of heroic/divine legitimacy is made explicit as he kills his cowardly son Calyphas:

> Here *loue*, receiue his fainting soule againe,
> A Forme not meet to giue that subiect essence,
> Whose matter is the flesh of *Tamburlain*,
> Wheren an incorporeall spirit mooues,
> Made of the mould whereof thy selfe consists,
> Which makes me valiant, proud, ambitious,
> Ready to leuie power against thy throne,
> That I might mooue the turning Spheares of heauen,
> For earth and al this aery region
> Cannot containe the state of *Tamburlaine*.
>
> (3785–94)

But for the last two lines, Tamburlaine might be saying what we generally recognize: that a worthy son has to go through a rebellion against his father. But for Marlowe, because there is no possibility of a father's or god's love across conflict, there can be no atonement such as can conclude filial rebellion, the son internalizing the father without needing to destroy him. As a consequence, paradoxically, Tamburlaine has no secure identity, except as his identity is to be forever taking over identity.

This uncertainty goes with Marlowe's riding on the power of his hero: clearly the play is based on an *unacknowledged* pact, the author's identification with the hero, for the enjoyment of *unacknowledged* magic. From this identification comes the manic power of the poetry. The author uses the play to persuade his audience to join him in the relationship with the hero. In the beginning, Theridamas, "Chiefest Captaine of *Mycetes* hoste" (66), sent to put down a Scythian shepherd turned bandit, sets the example as he exclaims:

Tamburlaine? A Scythian Shepheard, so imbellished
With Natures pride, and richest furniture,
His looks do menace heauen an dare the Gods. . . .

(350–52)

What stronge enchantments tice my yeelding soule?
. . . .
Won with thy words, & conquered with thy looks,
I yeeld my selfe, my men & horse to thee. . . .

(419, 423–24)

To reject the divine or take it over are, for Marlowe's sensibility
in a religiously structured culture, ways to a precarious liberation, confirmed in the theater by the audience. In Freudian
terms, again, the process provides release from a particularly
cruel superego by identification with a cruel figure of authority,
so that, instead of suffering cruelty, the threatened ego participates in the strong ideal figure's being cruel to others. Most of
the time it is with Tamburlaine in his cruel omnipotence that
we are led to identify by the moment by moment pulsating energy of the poetry, whatever our secondary responses of shock;
most of the time Tamburlaine threatens heaven and dares
the gods. When, alternatively, Tamburlaine claims sanction or
identity with God, it is a god "full of reuenging wrath" (4294)
sanctioning his sadism: "til by vision, or by speach I heare / Immortall *Ioue* say, Cease my *Tamburlaine,* / I will persist a terrour
to the world . . ." (3873–75). In projecting an alternative
world, centered on an Eastern, non-Christian conqueror who
had actually existed, whose conquests he follows on up-to-date
maps, and whose identity he aggrandizes by the alternative
supernatural of classical myth, Marlowe in *Tamburlaine* is leaving behind, as well as turning the tables on, the religious fear he
is to confront in *Doctor Faustus.*

Marlowe's man of war, as many have noted, is incon-
gruously poetical; though his "working woordes" as well as his
conquering sword are a practical means to power, he is devoted
as no man of action would be to verbal self-description and
self-assertion and the motor hallucination of gesture. And the
business of war, although it is relished in factual, up-to-date
technical terms, is presented chiefly as something to be *seen,*

threatening evidence of virility devoted to aggression: "Then shalt thou see the Scythian *Tamburlaine*, / Make but iest to win the Persean crowne" (802–3). Tamburlaine and his henchmen are manhood *on show.*

The special role that weaklings have in the play fits in with this use of the hero. Mycetes relishes the thought of the milk-white steeds of cavalry "Besmer'd with blood, that makes a dainty show" (88); but he depends utterly on his minister Meander to speak and act for him. In holding his inanity up to ridicule, the play presents and gets rid of a figure who might in effect parody something in its creator.[11] This potentiality comes out in the amusing exchange between Mycetes and Meander. After Meander in a large speech has used the story of "the cruell brothers of the earth, / Sprong of the teeth of Dragons venomous" (570–71), Mycetes asks:

> Was there such brethren, sweet *Meander,* say
> That sprong of teeth of Dragons venomous?
> MEANDER: So Poets say, my Lord.
> MYCETES: And tis a prety toy to be a Poet.
> Wel, wel (*Meander*) thou art deeply read:
> And hauing thee, I haue a iewell sure.
>
> (574–79)

If ever there was a poet determined not to be a toy, it was Christopher Marlowe.

In the new theater that Marlowe was using in a new way, a poet could, it seemed, be more than a toy. In the theater, Edward Alleyn could speak the lines usurping divinity, make the gestures confirming them, and have the support, in the process, of a mesmerized audience. In his book on group psychology, Freud explains the suggestibility and loss of moral inhibition in crowds by a leader's taking over temporarily the function

---

11. Constance Brown Kuriyama observes that Mycetes, weak, effeminate, and "discernibly enamored of Meander," enbodies a passive homosexual trend that Tamburlaine's violent assertion of manly power serves to deny (see *Hammer or Anvil: Psychological Patterns in Christopher Marlowe's Plays* [New Brunswick, N.J.: Rutgers University Press, 1981], p. 14).

of the superego.[12] Marlowe dramatizes Tamburlaine doing this for his followers, as first with Theridamas. There is even a scene where, during the vaunting before a battle, a former follower, now in the enemy camp and about to be rewarded there with a crown for his treason, asks Tamburlaine's permission to accept the crown (3618–36)! Marlowe was quoted by Baines as saying that "the first beginning of Religioun was only to keep men in awe."[13] Tamburlaine makes such a religion of himself. Freud likens the relation of a group with an effective leader to falling in love, where the beloved takes the place of the lover's ego ideal, and with it, not infrequently, much of the lover's moral sense. We can infer a liberating relation of this kind between Marlowe and his hero, as well as between the audience and the hero. Thus the theater is made of a kind of condenser: circuits are established that carry currents otherwise blocked by conscience, which makes cowards of us all.

This use of the theater not only develops new attitudes but permits the exploration of new knowledge. The hero worship liberates mind and imagination: energy normally locked up in maintaining inhibition or repression is freed for asserting and envisaging what would otherwise be unthinkable. Marlowe's poetic powers are freed to project a new vision of human possibilities. As the pact with Lucifer opens up the world to Faustus's elated imagination, so the dramatist's alliance with Tamburlaine permits Marlowe to envisage a new heaven, a new earth.

---

12. In *Group Psychology and the Analysis of the Ego*, Freud notes that often "when individuals come together in a group all their individual inhibitions fall away and all the cruel, brutal and destructive instincts . . . are stirred up to find free gratification" (*Standard Edition*, 18:79). He concludes that "the individual gives up his ego ideal and substitutes for it the group ideal as embodied in the leader" (18:129). The leader inherits his position psychologically from the authority of the father as experienced in early childhood; ultimately, for Freud, "the leader of the group is still the dreaded primal father. . . . The primal father is the group ideal, which governs in the place of the ego ideal" (18:127).

13. In the "note containing the opinion of one Christopher Marly Concerning his damnable Iudgment of Religion, and scorn of Gods world," which summarizes Baines's accusations in the 1593 investigation of Marlowe by the Privy Council. This note is reprinted in Appendix 1 in Steane, *Marlowe: A Critical Study*, pp. 363–64.

"*conceiuing and subduing both*"

But there is a drastic limitation on this liberation. Nothing can be envisaged except as it aggrandizes the hero's identity. Otherness is a challenge which must either be incorporated or destroyed. This becomes clearest in the second part, as we shall see. The first part has a clear overall structure which one can characterize as a do-it-yourself "family romance." Tamburlaine does not discover that he is of royal birth or a demigod produced by one of Zeus's by-blows; instead the birth of the hero happens by his making himself a god on earth. The invented role of Zenocrate, for which there was no basis in Marlowe's sources, provides the center for the triumphant finale of Tamburlaine's self-creation in *Part 1*. The play introduces its hero as he captures the Egyptian princess; his conquests make good his promise to be a monarch worthy of her before he marries her; it concludes with his crowning her and leading her off to their rites of marriage as "*Tamburlaine* takes truce with al the world" (2311). It thus has a satisfying heroic structure which writes large the fantasy of achieving virtual omnipotence.

At the close there is a self-proclaimed apotheosis, as Tamburlaine justifies his suit to Zenocrate to her captured father, the Egyptian Souldane:

> The God of war resignes his roume to me,
> Meaning to make me Generall of the world,
> *Ioue* viewing me in armes, lookes pale and wan,
> Fearing my power should pull him from his throne.
> Where ere I come the fatall sisters sweat,
> . . . .
> Millions of soules sit on the bankes of *Styx*,
> . . . .
> And see my Lord, a sight of strange import,
> Emperours and kings lie breathlesse at my feet,
> The Turk and his great Emperesse
> . . . .
> With them *Arabia* too hath left his life,
> Al sights of power to grace my victory.
> (2232–36, 2245, 2250–52, 2255–56)

Destructiveness is taken by Tamburlaine, as always, to be the essential proof of manhood—"His honor, that consists in sheading blood" (2259). He has taken over the role of the god of war and daunted Jove himself. The assumption that has been writ large is that to be a man—to be worthy of the ideal woman—it is necessary to be a god, or like a god, and cruel in that omnipotence. The destructive power that is feared as punishment for rivalry is taken as proof of manhood. For good measure, the bride's father, once conquered, is handsomely promised augmented dominions.

It is striking evidence of the power of the incest taboo, and of Marlowe's integrity as an artist, that the sexual conquest or possession of Zenocrate by Tamburlaine is never actually envisaged. In creating Zenocrate's role out of whole cloth, he was of course drawing on traditions of courtly love poetry in which worshipful love is often associated with displaced expression of taboo. But everything in Marlowe's play is consistent with his presenting in the relation of Tamburlaine to Zenocrate a romance that seeks to extend or recover essential qualities of a relationship with a mother. His hero chastely cherishes his captured princess—squires her about to the point where *she* is desperate with frustration (see 1006–9). The marriage takes place offstage. Meanwhile he has spoken exquisite love poetry, the most striking of which is literally frigid:

> With milke-white Hartes vpon an Iuorie sled,
> Thou shalt be drawen amidst the frosen Pooles,
> And scale the ysie mountaines lofty tops.
>
> (294–96)

Tamburlaine's indifference and cruelty to other women are consistent with the unpossessable nature his love imparts to Zenocrate, her eyes "Wounding the world with woonder and with loue" (3050). In *Part 1*, Marlowe's expression of the two attitudes in his hero strikingly juxtaposes them. Shortly after Tamburlaine has suggested to starving Bajazeth that he eat his queen—"Here is my dagger, dispatch her while she is fat" (1687)—and immediately after he has sent the virgins of Damascus to die on the lances of his cavalry, he comes forward to speak the great and strange soliloquy occasioned by Zenocrate's plea that he spare her father and his Egypt. The shift from an exhibition of impervious, constructed manhood to a revelation of suffering about beauty is a stroke of genius—genius moving, not quite certainly, towards fuller, more inclusive expression.

> Ah faire *Zenocrate*, diuine *Zenocrate*,
> Faire is too foule an Epithite for thee,
> That in thy passion for thy countries loue,
> And feare to see thy kingly Fathers harme,
> With haire discheweld wip'st thy watery cheeks.
>
> (1916–20)

There is a curious movement in the extraordinary passage these lines open. It slides from the conflict about sparing the Souldane to a more fundamental conflict underlying Tamburlaine's worship of Zenocrate, and in doing so shifts into terms as appropriate to Marlowe as to his hero:

> neither Perseans Soueraign, nor the Turk
> Troubled my sences with conceit of foile,
> So much by much, as dooth *Zenocrate*.
> What is beauty saith my sufferings then?
>
> (1938–41)

The fear attaching to Zenocrate becomes explicit in these lines. The passage which follows about poetry is about the problem of possessing Zenocrate; it comes explicitly in response to the suffering of senses troubled by "conceit of foile." The possession envisaged by poetry is in imagery of feeding which first emphasizes a constraint felt upon the autarchy of the poet:

> If all the pens that euer poets held,
> Had fed the feeling of their maisters thoughts,
> . . . .
> Yet should ther houer in their restlesse heads,
> One thought, one grace, one woonder at the least,
> Which into words no vertue can digest.
>
> (1942–43, 1952–54)

As Tamburlaine pulls himself back after this momentary surrender to beauty, we can glimpse a source of the compulsion, in Marlowe's sensibility, to express power and beauty in terms of domination. Tamburlaine breaks off by exclaiming that it is "vnseemly" "for my Sex, . . . / My nature and the terrour of my name, / To harbour thoughts effeminate and faint" (1955, 1957–58). In justification, he turns from Zenocrate to contemplation of himself in terms of the Renaissance ideal of the complete man: "euery warriour" devoted to fame and victory "Must needs haue beauty beat on his conceites." He concludes with the attitude of the line quoted at the head of this section:

> I thus conceiuing and subduing both
>
> . . . .
>
> Shal giue the world to note for all my byrth
> That Vertue solely is the sum of glorie,
> And fashions men with true nobility.
>
> (1964, 1969–71)

The problem at the center of the soliloquy—the problem of loving—is left behind in self-contemplation centering on his own *vertu* or force as a power capable of subjugating what his imagination can conceive. Having opened up this suffering, Marlowe can but close over it again—and send his hero back to bullying Bajazeth.

"I thus conceiuing and subduing both" summarizes the action of the sensibility which creates *Tamburlaine*. It suggests the play's basic limitation—its overriding of irony, its compulsive domineering which finally becomes tiresome, even though poetry and theatrical imagination are remarkably sustained through both parts. The one great exception to the absence of tragic irony about the hero is the death of Zenocrate in *Part 2*. It provides a situation in which Marlowe can dramatize fully Tamburlaine's paradoxical dependence on her. The scene is constructed with splendid symmetry: static figures—three physicians, three warrior companions, three sons—are disposed around Zenocrate's bed of state to set off Tamburlaine's passionate movement. Everything turns on the moment when "*The musicke sounds, and she dies.*"

What concerns me here is the way the scene extends the rhythm of "conceiving" and "subduing." It opens with the most enlarged conceiving of Zenocrate, shifts after her death to the expression of extreme anguish of frustration, and then recovers with a characteristic subduing, by domineering, of the anguish of conceiving. Thus we can see in it both the creativity of the impulse to worship that Marlowe expresses and also the limitation that vulnerability in suffering beauty involves for him.

Tamburlaine begins his lament by describing Zenocrate as the source, now darkening, of all light and life, and then goes on to the superb lyric which describes the prospect of her assumption into heaven:

> Now walk the angels on the walles of heauen,
> As Centinels to warne th' immortall soules,
> To entertaine deuine *Zenocrate.*
>
> (2983–85)

In the beautiful lines which follow, there is, for once, deep reverence and a loss of self in contemplation of the harmony of the universe. Instead of appropriating the cosmos to aggrandize his identity, Tamburlaine envisages for a moment welcome into heaven:

> The Cherubins and holy Seraphins
> That sing and play before the king of kings,
> Vse all their voices and their instruments
> To entertaine diuine *Zenocrate.*
> And in this sweet and currious harmony,
> The God that tunes this musicke to our soules:
> Holds out his hand in highest maiesty
> To entertaine diuine *Zenocrate.*
>
> (2994–3001)

Of course in making Zenocrate's death equivalent to the Assumption of the Virgin Mary, the lines on one side are blasphemous, and characteristically aggressive. But Marlowe's sensibility is reaching, through the figure of Zenocrate, out beyond the limitation of violence. Tamburlaine ends his speech by asking that an ecstasy take him up to heaven and end his life with Zenocrate's:

> Then let some holy trance conuay my thoughts,
> Vp to the pallace of th' imperiall heauen:

That this my life may be as short to me
As are the daies of sweet *Zenocrate.*

(3002-5)

In expressing, through Zenocrate, something like religious
awe, this beautiful poetry fits with a view that it is initially
through the figures of the parents, godlike, as experienced in
infancy, that men reach toward society's conceptions of divinity. Such a view need not deny the objective reality of the
transcendent forces to which a mature worship responds. The
parents after all themselves depend, in their creative and nurturing role, on forces and realities which transcend their individuality. Filial piety, in a successful development, goes beyond
the parents to become a larger social and/or religious piety,
whatever the forms under which it is envisaged. The Oedipus
complex, in this perspective, appears as the route through
which a child's worship may develop into a man's, or else be
blocked or distorted. Tamburlaine's celebration of Zenocrate,
and the impulse which goes with it to lose himself, with her, in
the "currious harmony" of divinity, need not be reduced, by for-
mula, to "nothing but the expression of oedipal feelings." The
poetry captures, through her, actual majesty of the universe,
whether in the imagery of light in the opening cosmological
celebration of her eyes, or in the neo-Christian imagery of the
assumption lyric.

After the pause when *"The musicke sounds, and she dies,"*
the same basic idea of her assumption into heaven is expressed
in classical rather than Christian imagery, with an opposite emphasis, on jealousy and deprivation. Tamburlaine commands his
followers to

Raise Caualieros higher than the cloudes,
And with the cannon breake the frame of heauen
. . . .
For amorous *Ioue* hath snatcht my loue from hence,
Meaning to make her stately Queene of heauen.

(3071-72, 3075-76)

The pleading lines which follow are shouted upward:

> What God so euer holds thee in his armes,
> Giuing thee Nectar and Ambrosia,
> Behold me here diuine *Zenocrate*,
> Rauing, impatient, desperate and mad,
> . . . .
> And if thou pitiest *Tamburlain* the great,
> Come downe from heauen and liue with me againe.
>
> (3077–80, 3085–86)

There is dramatic, ironic perspective here as nowhere else in *Tamburlaine*. Marlowe's mighty line is being used not to flatter expectations of omnipotence but to confront the irony that human finitude goes with such expectations. Where regularly the stage is used to confirm the hyperbolic, here the physical situation, the shouting up at heaven, enforces the irony. "What God so euer holds thee in his armes, / Giuing thee Nectar and Ambrosia," has a poignancy consistent with what underlies the whole drama. Nowhere is there any cue for an embrace of pleasure of Tamburlaine with Zenocrate: only a god can *enjoy* her; and Tamburlaine here finds that, despite all his titanic efforts, he is not a god. Amorous Jove has won out after all.

Tamburlaine recovers himself, subdues what he has conceived, by turning to the dead body:

> Though she be dead, yet let me think she liues,
> And feed my mind that dies for want of her:
> Where ere her soule be, thou shalt stay with me
> Embalm'd with Cassia, Amber Greece and Myrre,
> Not lapt in lead but in a sheet of gold,
> And till I die thou shalt not be interr'd.
>
> (3095–3100)

There is an ominous suggestion of breaking through the forbidden as Tamburlaine addresses the body: "thou shalt stay with me. . . ." We feel the troubling fusion of symbolic life and literal death which skirts all funerals and comes into its own with necrophilia. Tamburlaine covers over this dreadfulness with a sheet of gold, and goes on to solace himself by burning the town: "The houses burnt, wil looke as if they mourn'd" (3107).

The whole business of carrying Zenocrate's gold-enclosed body about with him is an exact symbolic expression of fixation.

"And make whole cyties caper in the aire"

Where Tamburlaine envisages the possibility of reaching "th'-imperiall heauen" with Zenocrate by dying in an ecstasy, "some holy trance," we have a version of Faustus's more desperate and immediate "Sweete *Helen,* make me immortall with a kisse: / Her lips suckes forth my soule, see where it flies . . ." (1330–31).[14] Where Helen is dramatized as an alternative to heavenly joys denied Faustus by God's wrath, the positive side of Tamburlaine's ambivalence can envisage for a moment a "God that tunes this musicke to our soules," welcoming Zenocrate. But Zenocrate, though she has a generous feminine concern for his safety in war and intercedes with him for her sons when he has doubts that they are effeminate, is *not* envisaged as an intercessor for Tamburlaine with God.

Her concern that he should go on living after her death is expressed in very moving poetry:

> TAMBURLAINE: Liue still my Loue and so conserue my life,
>   Or dieng, be the author of my death.
> ZENOCRATE: Liue still my Lord, O let my soueraigne lieu,
>
> · · · · · · · · · · · · · · · · · · · ·
>
>   But let me die my Loue, yet let me die,
>   With loue and patience let your true loue die:

14. In response to her dying, Tamburlaine imagines that Zenocrate, "had she liu'd before the siege of *Troy,*" would have displaced Helen in "Homers Iliads: / Her name had bene in euery line he wrote . . ." (3054, 3057–58). His evocation of the destructive power of Helen, "whose beauty sommond Greece to armes, / And drew a thousand ships to Tenedos" (3055–56), looks toward Faustus's: "Was this the face that lancht a thousand shippes? / And burnt the toplesse Towres of Ilium?" (*Faus.* 1328–29). In *Doctor Faustus,* however, the protagonist's surrender to Helen is part of the overall ironic design of the tragedy; it dramatizes not only the impulse toward dependence in Tamburlaine's idealized relation to Zenocrate but also, as we shall see in the next chapter, its self-destructive implications. The whole thrust of *Tamburlaine,* the author's relationship to his hero, requires that all irony, except at moments we have noted, should be at others' expense, not the hero's.

Your griefe and furie hurtes my second life,
Yet let me kisse my Lord before I die,
And let me die with kissing of my Lord.

(3023–25, 3034–38)

The rocking motion of phrases echoed or reiterated is even more effective when the lines are read in place within the whole dying speech. The rocking cherishing goes back, I think, to the earliest relationship with the mother. But, though it labors the obvious to say so, there is nothing of the Holy Mother as intercessor because, on the other side of the ambivalence, Zenocrate is not immaculate with "amorous *Ioue*." As Tamburlaine imagines a god "feeding her nectar," he is in Hamlet's position protesting Gertrude's "honeying and making love / Over the nasty sty." But part of the profound difference between Marlowe's and Shakespeare's sensibilities is that Marlowe not only cannot envisage atonement with the father or Father, he also cannot entertain identification with feminine responses, with the mother—except as emasculation or ravishment.[15] Later plays, *Doctor Faustus* and especially of course *Edward II*, explore being ravished by figures of power. In *Tamburlaine* the author is committed to a hero who defends against it by doing all the ravishing himself.

Constance Brown Kuriyama, in her psychoanalytic study of the plays as the unfolding expression of Marlowe's homosexuality, explores the ramifications of what she characterizes as *Tamburlaine*'s strategy of massive denial of passivity. She sees the strategy of denial as a program carried through from the first play to the sequel; but in her view the second part involves increasing ambivalence in the author about his titanic hero, because where in the first Tamburlaine is a rebel, in the second he has become the established figure of authority, and so threaten-

15. See Michael Goldman, "Marlowe and the Histrionics of Ravishment," in *Two Renaissance Mythmakers: Christopher Marlowe and Ben Jonson*, ed. Alvin Kernan, Selected Papers from the English Institute, 1975–76 (Baltimore: Johns Hopkins University Press, 1977), pp. 22–40. Goldman explores "the immense instabilities of ravishment" that animate "a distinctive stance toward the world" from which "all of Marlowe's drama flows" (pp. 40, 36).

ing as well as fascinating for Marlowe.[16] She links this shift in Marlowe's relation to Tamburlaine to the opposition that breaks the surface in the cowardly son Calyphas, whose role wavers: sometimes he is contemptibly comic; sometimes he effectually expresses hedonistic independence. After Tamburlaine's exhortation to his sons on martial discipline, Calyphas's "My Lord, but this is dangerous to be done" (3283) is laughable. But his later, fuller statements have validity as a critical response: "I take no pleasure to be murtherous, / Nor care for blood when wine wil quench my thirst" (3702–3).

There is, certainly, a moment that moves in the direction of Falstaff's "The better part of valor is discretion, in the which better part I have sav'd my life" (*1 H 4* 5.4.119–21). As his eager brothers go off to battle, Calyphas says

> Take you the honor, I will take my ease,
> My wisedome shall excuse my cowardise:
> I goe into the field before I need?
> The bullets fly at random where they list.
>
> (3722–25)

"Here's no scoring but upon the pate" (*1H4* 5.3.31–32). But where Falstaff starts up alive after his mock death, Calyphas is dragged out after the battle, speechless with terror through thirty lines until his father righteously stabs him. Marlowe has no room—such as there had been in *Dido* and will be, in plenty, in *The Jew of Malta*—for full comic détente. Though he can dramatize alternatives to Tamburlaine, it is only for his hero savagely to quell them.

This is far more often the case with moral rather than hedonistic criticism. What chiefly happens in *Part 2*, as I see it, and what most disturbs us, is an all but overt plunge into homosexual sadism under the guise of martial prowess, after the etiology of Marlowe's kind of homosexuality has been presented in the

16. Kuriyama opens her chapter on the two plays by exhibiting quite exhaustively the disagreements of critics, then surveys surface inconsistencies of the plays, notably Tamburlaine's now defying, now co-opting the gods. Her telling psychological analysis brings out imagery of phallic competition and of emasculation, or again of threats in anal-sadistic modes, which I am neglecting here. See *Hammer or Anvil*, pp. 1–52.

death of Zenocrate. Her picture is set up in his tent. Why? Because her

> looks will shed such influence in my campe,
> As if *Bellona,* Goddesse of the war
> Threw naked swords and sulphur bals of fire,
> Upon the heads of all our enemies.
>
> (3229–32)

The sons' continuing grieving is cut short by their father setting out "to teach you rudiments of war: / Ile haue you learn to sleepe vpon the ground, / March in your armour throwe watery Fens . . ." (3244–46). J. B. Steane has a telling comment on lines which soon follow in this speech. He observes, correctly I think (as almost always with Steane), that

> the writing is remarkably even throughout both parts: in only a very few places has the imagination gone dead. Often there is an exhilaration rare in poetry, carried by the span of images, thrust of verbs, boldness of hyperbole and the confident balance and long stride of the rhetoric. A brief example:
>
> > Besiege a fort, to vndermine a towne,
> > And make whole cyties caper in the aire.
> >
> > (3250–51)
>
> It is the verb "caper" which stamps these lines as Marlovian. Not simply vigorous hyperbole, the word is a microcosmic sample of the prevailing spirit: make them caper; prod them with your aggressive vitality; blow them sky-high and they can dance to your tune up there.[17]

17. *Marlowe: A Critical Study,* p. 109. Steane's is by all odds the best literary study of Marlowe's whole works, their powers and limitations, that I know, a book to complement Harry Levin's landmark *The Overreacher: A Study of Christopher Marlowe* (Cambridge, Mass.: Harvard University Press, 1952), with its wider exhibition of the poet's relationship to intellectual and moral currents of his age. But Steane sees the mind of the author of *Tamburlaine* as divided in a different way than I do, on moral lines: "evil . . . gloried in, though opposed fitfully by the misgivings . . . of normal moral judgment" (p. 112). My structural and psychological analysis is on different lines, but I admire greatly Steane's understanding of the play's qualities, including especially its special kind of religious feeling.

Steane does not add that this image makes the cities equivalent to the victims of homoerotic torment, patsies subjected to sadistic teasing. The brutal treatment of the Turkish concubines of course fits with this alternative erotic release.

Many critics assume that the outrageousness of Tamburlaine's actions undercuts the glowing words, especially in this second part, where after Zenocrate's death his cruelties become in their eyes maniacal. Douglas Cole, acknowledging that "the ambitious rebel, a figure consistently vilified in the academic tragedies and other orthodox sources, is . . . brought to final exaltation" in the first part, would like to see the physical violence of the second part as ironic comment. But he can find no textual basis, and so must conclude lamely that "if the irony of such juxtaposition is not intended, it represents a serious dramatic error."[18] To speak of "a dramatic *error*" is surely inappropriate, for Marlowe has gone out of his way to *include* moral condemnation and then quite literally—and sadistically—to stifle it. Before the captive kings are hitched to the chariot, they each revile Tamburlaine in turn, as a damned monster, a fiend of hell, calling on Radamanth and Eacus to revenge his outrages, most immediately the killing of his own son. Tamburlaine's reponse needs to be quoted in full to get clear the way Marlowe has him put down the moral protest and soar out above it:

> Wel, bark ye dogs. Ile bridle al your tongues
> And bind them close with bits of burnisht steele,
> Downe to the channels of your hatefull throats,
> And with the paines my rigour shall inflict,
> Ile make ye roare, that earth may eccho foorth
> The far resounding torments ye sustaine,
> As when an heard of lusty Cymbrian Buls,
> Run mourning round about the Femals misse,
> And stung with furie of their following,
> Fill all the aire with troublous bellowing:
> I will with Engines, neuer exercisde,
> Conquer, sacke, and vtterly consume
> Your cities and your golden pallaces,

18. *Suffering and Evil in the Plays of Christopher Marlowe* (Princeton, N.J.: Princeton University Press, 1962), pp. 102, 108.

And with the flames that beat against the clowdes
Incense the heauens, and make the starres to melt,
As if they were the teares of *Mahomet*
For hot consumption of his countries pride:
And til by vision, or by speech I heare
Immortall *Ioue* say, Cease my *Tamburlaine*,
I will persist a terrour to the world,
Making the Meteors, that like armed men
Are seene to march vpon the towers of heauen,
Run tilting round about the firmament,
And breake their burning Lances in the aire,
For honor of my woondrous victories.

(3856–80)

There is a special appropriateness to the burnished steel
bits which bridle tongues "Downe to the channels of your
hatefull throats," for it is just this area that gives Tamburlaine
important satisfactions. It is crucial that Tamburlaine's vaunting does *not* fall over into huff-snuff bombast, despite the drastic
things it is drawing us in to feel with it. The passage echoes
Spenser's *Faerie Queene,* with a difference, in its description of
the resounding torments. In Spenser, it is Orgoglio, Pride, who
bellows, as Arthur rescues the Red Cross Knight from him:

He lowdly brayd with beastly yelling sownd,
That all the fieldes rebellowed againe;
As great a noyse, as when in Cymbrian plaine
An heard of Bulles, whom kindly rage doth sting,
Do for the milky mothers want complaine,
And fill the fieldes with troublous bellowing:
The neighbor woods around with hollow murmur ring.

(1.8.11)

In Marlowe it is Pride who inflicts the pain instead of receiving
it. Another contrast is the way Spenser's "kindly rage" and
"milky mothers" make the sexual striving of the bulls part of the
natural cycle, the bulls impatient because the cows are still with
their new calves, where Marlowe's bulls, "stung with furie," run
around about an empty center, "the Femals misse."

But the center is not empty in the finale of rhapsodic destruction which next is generated from Tamburlaine's "I will."

As he promises to use "Engines, neuer exercisde" to "vttrly con-
sume" the Turkish cities, one remembers the firestorms of the
Second World War, produced by engines never exercised in
Marlowe's time. Marlowe's fascination with technology, however, is inseparable from a human and mythological vision of
the universe, so that the firestorms have cosmological and
bodily results:

> with flames that beat against the clowdes
> Incense the heauens, and make the starres to melt,
> As if they were the teares of Mahomet
> For hot consumption of his countries pride: . . .

The next moment, after this defiance of "the heauens," glories
in the sanction of "immortall *Ioue*," Marlowe characteristically
having it both ways. The anguished circling of the bellowing
bulls at the outset is matched by an exultant dance of meteors at
the close: it is on Tamburlaine that they center as "like armed
men" they

> Run tilting round about the firmament,
> And breake their burning Lances in the aire,
> For honor of my woondrous victories.

Tamburlaine's narcissism, here as elsewhere, is the fulfillment of his violence—"Wherein as in a mirrour may be seene, /
His honor, that consists in sheading blood" (2258–59). If we
look back behind the dramatic construction, the narcissism is a
recourse in the predicament of not being able to love, as the
violence is a massive defense against fear of retaliation, which
also blocks love. The only object left for love is himself.[19]
(There is a certain superflux available for his henchmen, because they are *his*.) We can note that through the relationship
of identification, the hero's narcissism is the poet's giving up
himself to his hero. In considering the street brawls in which
Marlowe was involved, Kuriyama reviews the evidence suggest-
ing a provocative manner—aggressively scornful of others, en-

---

19. See Freud, "On Narcissism: An Introduction," *Standard Edition*,
14:73–102.

amored of itself—that contemporaries might well have found insufferable. She notes that the poem attached to Gabriel Harvey's *New Letter of Notable Contents* "seems to corroborate" other accounts of Marlowe's personality: Harvey describes the recently dead Marlowe as Juno's peacock, with "toade Conceit" and "tamberlaine contempt," a man who "nor feared God, nor dreaded Diu'll / Nor ought admired, but his wondrous selfe."[20] In Kuriyama's speculations, aggression and narcissism play themselves out with deflating circularity: violently impulsive efforts to defend against threats to vulnerable self-regard characteristically collapse into "ambivalence toward violence, augmented by guilt"—a sequence that "occurs repeatedly in Marlowe's works," as well as in "episodes in Marlowe's life" (p. 231). But in the meteors' dance, Tamburlaine's self-love is confirmed cosmologically—and by armed men who break *their* lances in honor of his potency! It is not fair, we must note, to say that Marlowe could not admire anything but "his wondrous selfe"— he could create and admire Tamburlaine.

A "propheticall full mouth," "bred in Merlin's Race"

In insisting on the way the immense poetic power draws us in to participate in such passages, I do not mean to imply that we cannot detach ourselves from them after the initial experience. Presumably we can do so the more easily because we do not live in the society in which they were written, with its established worshipful structure, secular and religious. There is not the heady release for us that these plays must have offered their original audiences. And of course Marlowe's contemporaries were perfectly capable of detachment, in response to shock, or defense against it, as witness the phrases from Robert Greene which I quote in the subhead for this section. Greene's characterizations of Marlowe (the first phrase was published in 1588, when *Tamburlaine* was fire-new) not only distance him, but make the point that the complex new amalgam of energies he dealt in could be seen as a version of extremist Protestant

20. *Hammer or Anvil*, p. 224; Harvey's poem is reprinted in Brooke, *The Life of Marlowe and the Tragedy of Dido Queen of Carthage* (London: Methuen, 1930), pp. 111–12.

"prophesying." Tamburlaine is animated, in effect, by a violently antinomian sense of "election."

Though he is not acting on behalf of a religious sect, he is a one-man sect, his own "Scourge of God" sect. The chief basis in the text for Battenhouse's strange reading of the play as "a grandly moral spectacle" is that, as he notes, Tamburlaine refers to himself as the Scourge of God no less than twelve times.[21] But it was normally moralists *on the outside* of the political process who, from Isaiah 10 on down, used the idea of a ruler being the scourge of God for sins of a people. Sixteenth-century histories did make mention of Tamburlaine's having spoken of himself as the "ire" or "wrath" of God. Battenhouse points out that in Thomas Fortescue's translation of Pedro Maxia (a principal source, probably, for Marlowe), Tamburlaine is included as an exemplar in a section entitled "How for the most parte, cruel kings and bloody tirants are the Ministers of God, and how notwithstanding they continually end in state of most wretched and extreme misery." As "ministers," they "are instruments wherewith God chastiseth sin, as also with the same approoueth and tryeth the just."[22] Instead of emphasizing his hero's instrumentality, Marlowe, by his poetry, goes *inside* this role of tyrant, and does without any "just" who are tried.[23] He follows the historians in showing Tamburlaine dying a natural death among his children and friends—*not* conforming to the moralists' generalization that tyrants "continually end in state most wretched and extreme misery"—with no intimation that the death is a retribution.[24]

There is much in Tamburlaine's sense of election that reminds one of religious violence in the Reformation period,

21. See *Marlowe's Tamburlaine*, p. 133.

22. Ibid., p. 13.

23. An exception to this is Olympia in *Part 2*, but her fidelity in love, not faith, is tried not by Tamburlaine, but by Theridamas, and she rather spectacularly refuses her reward.

24. Here my sense of the meaning agrees with Paul Kocher's (*Christopher Marlowe: A Study of his Thought, Learning, and Character* [Chapel Hill: University of North Carolina Press, 1946], pp. 90–95), and not (as usually) with Steane's. See Steane, pp. 114–15 and note, where Kocher's argument is quoted briefly and countered.

when scrupulous, God-fearing men turned their aggression into doing God's will to his enemies. This is nowhere clearer than in the burning of the *Alcoran*:

> TECHELLES: What shal be done with their wiues and children my Lord.
> TAMBURLAINE: *Techelles,* drowne them all, man, woman, and child,
> Leaue not a Babylonian in the towne.
> TECHELLES: I will about it straight, come Souldiers.   *Exit.*
> TAMBURLAINE: Now *Casane,* wher's the Turkish *Alcaron,*
> And all the heapes of supersticious bookes,
> Found in the Temples of that *Mahomet,*
> Whom I haue thought of God? they shal be burnt.
> VSUMCASANE: Here they are my Lord.
> TAMBURLAINE: Wel said, let there be a fire presently.
> *(They light a fire.)*
> In vaine I see men worship *Mahomet.*
> My sword hath sent millions of Turks to hell,
> Slew all his Priests, his kinsmen, and his friends,
> And yet I liue vntoucht by *Mahomet:*
> There is a God full of reuenging wrath,
> From whom the thunder and the lightning breaks,
> Whose Scourge I am, and him will I obey
> So *Casane,* fling them in the fire.
> *(They burn the books.)*
> Now *Mahomet,* if thou haue any power,
> Come downe thy selfe and worke a myracle,
> Thou art not woorthy to be worshipped,
> That suffers flames of fire to burne the writ
> Wherein the sum of thy religion rests.
> Why send'st thou not a furious whyrlwind downe,
> To blow thy Alcaron vp to thy throne,
> Where men report, thou sitt'st by God himselfe,
> Or vengeance on the head of *Tamburlain,*
> That shakes his sword against thy maiesty,
> And spurns the Abstracts of thy foolish lawes.
> Wel souldiers, *Mahomet* remaines in hell,
> He cannot heare the voice of *Tamburlain,*
> Seeke out another Godhead to adore,
> The God that sits in heauen, if any God,
> For he is God alone, and none but he.
>
> (4280–4313)

As Greenblatt observes, a sixteenth-century audience would be far from being shocked by the burning of Muhammadan holy writ.[25] And Marlowe has covered the skeptical defiance (which even echoes the jibe at Christ to come down from the cross!) by the suggestion that Tamburlaine is converting away from Islam, ready to "Seeke out another Godhead"—though "if any God" can be read two ways, as a skeptical interjection, or as permission to the soldiers to let the search alone if they choose. The total massacre which the prophesying justifies may seem mere theatrical brutality—until we remember that the Massacre of Paris had already taken place, with others less famous, and that the Thirty Years War was soon to follow (beginning with the theological argument in Prague that led to "defenestration" of one side as prologue to massacres). The "final solutions" of our own time were to follow also.

Reggie Reed has related *Tamburlaine* to the English Puritan practice and doctrine of "prophesying" in the 1570s and 1580s, including the controversies, centered at Marlowe's Cambridge, over the official Anglican prohibitions of the practice.[26] By doing so, she brings out affinities between Tamburlaine's sense of election and the energy and commitment of radical reformers with whom Marlowe (on an Archbishop Parker scholarship to read for holy orders) certainly had contact, whatever his attitudes and relations. Theridamas, overwhelmed by the Scythian shepherd's eloquence, says "Not *Hermes* Prolocutor to the Gods, / Could vse perswasions more patheticall" (405–6). The whole effect, Reed suggests, has affinities to the Calvinist prophesyings, where "the Prolocutor was the first and main speaker" and the faithful laity also took part, according to "the text of St. Paul

---

25. *Renaissance Self-Fashioning*, p. 202.
26. Reed quotes (from William Pierce, *An Historical Introduction to the Marprelate Tracts* [London: Constable, 1908], p. 142) a 1587 tract by Cambridge-trained John Bridges: "The [prophesying] Preacher respecteth God, and all the people are the hearers of God, speaking unto them by him, *Qui loquitur loquatur eloquia Dei*." I am drawing on an abbreviated version of Reed's unpublished doctoral dissertation (State University of New York at Buffalo, 1970) which she has kindly furnished me. Her work has ably opened up an important, previously unexplored historical context of Marlowe's *Tamburlaine*.

'For all ye may prophesy one by one, that all may learn, and all may be comforted'" (1 Cor. 14.31). Reed notes how Anglican objections to the Puritan practice focused on its antinomian tendencies. Tyndale at the end of his translation of Genesis explained that divine command can overrule law: "Jacob robbed Laban his uncle; Moses robbed the Egyptians; Abraham is about to slay and burn his own son: and all are holy works, because they are wrought in faith at God's commandment."[27] Richard Hooker argues against this strain in the English Puritans by the example of the Anabaptists, who "were grown at last to think they could not offer unto God more acceptable sacrifice, than by turning their adversaries clean out of house and home, and by enriching themselves with all kind of spoil and pillage; which being laid to their charge, they had in readiness their answer, that now the time was come when according to our Savior's promise, 'the meek ones must inherit the earth,' and that their title thereunto was the same which the righteous Israelites had unto the goods of the wicked Egyptians."[28]

It is not such a long way from the Scythian Shepherd to John of Leyden. Although there was no even faintly comparable violence from the English conventicles in the sixteenth century, their excited energy and the controversy about their radical Protestant claims provide a way of more fully understanding Greene's reference to Marlowe in *Menaphon* as "some propheticall full mouth" and his scornful involuntary tribute in *Perimedes*, where again "prophetical" characterizes the rival dramatist: "Latelye two Gentlemen Poets, made two mad men of Rome . . . had it in derision, for that I could not make my verses iet vpon the stage in tragicall buskins, euerie worde filling the mouth like the faburden of Bo-Bell, daring God out of heauen with that Atheist *Tamburlan,* or blaspheming with the mad preest of the sonne: but let me rather openly pocket vp the Asse at *Diogenes* hand: then wantonlye set out such impious instances of intolerable poetrie: such mad and scoffing poets, that haue propheticall spirits, as bred in *Merlins* race, if there be anye in England that set the end of scollarisme in an English

27. Quoted in Reed.
28. Preface, chap. 8, *Of the Laws of Ecclesiastical Polity,* in *Works,* ed. John Keble, vol. 1 (Oxford University Press, 1837); quoted by Reed.

blanck verse."[29] As a further link between the theological ardor of the early conventicles and prophetical *Tamburlaine*, one has only to remember that the separatist seeds flowered later in the power of Milton's poetry—and recall Cromwell's Ironsides as they charged into battle singing a psalm.

Steane responds to the religious feeling of many passages to conclude that, while the play reflects a somewhat "divided mind" in Marlowe, Tamburlaine worships "an unnamed God of power and beauty," immanent as "a dynamic rather than a moral force." "The mind which postulates this divine vigour also places at the head of humanity the man with most vitality," so that "Tamburlaine becomes a religious symbol. It is the fact that what he embodies touches religious depths in Marlowe that gives these plays that poise, confidence, stamina and solidity which is theirs in notable contrast to his other works."[30] This account, as always with Steane, is responsive and illuminating. But it notably fails to explain the positive role of pleasure in cruelty and neglects the frequent reversals by which Tamburlaine threatens and defies the divine with which at other moments he identifies. To understand more fully the powerful energies at work in *Tamburlaine* and Tamburlaine, we have had to shift our ground and ask what the play does for its author, what enters into the process of creation which we experience.

Greenblatt's chapter on Marlowe, especially when read in the context of *Renaissance Self-Fashioning*, with its sense of the desperation that attended new modes of improvising identity, brings out more fully than any previous study the dramatist's staggering exhibition of the violence and self-destructiveness of his age. Greenblatt brings to bear a wide, unflinching knowledge of the ruthlessness—courtly, colonial, religious—which the period's ideologies both hide and protect.[31] In his view, Marlowe, though involved by his own destructive and self-

---

29. *Life and Works of Robert Greene*, ed. A. B. Grosart, 12 vols. (London: The Heath Library, 1881–83), 6:86, 7:7–8. The passage from *Menaphon* points at Marlowe by alluding to his birthplace and his father's occupation as a cobbler, as J. H. Ingram first observed in *Christopher Marlowe and His Associates* (1904; reprint New York: Cooper Square, 1970), pp. 118–19.

30. *Marlowe: A Critical Study*, pp. 114–16.

destructive needs in all his works, is at the same time master-fully detached in all of them, including *Tamburlaine*. Kuriyama, who focuses on the cruelty within the dynamics of the author rather than of the times, sees a progress in self-knowledge, awe-some and finally poignant. About the relation of the works to the man, I agree with her view.[32]

We have seen how much that was alive in the age, not or-dinarily fully acknowledged, is expressed in *Tamburlaine*. Mar-lowe's use of the theater not only develops new attitudes but permits the exploration of new knowledge. His poetic powers are freed to project a new version of human values and possibili-ties. The hero worship liberates mind and imagination: energy normally locked up in maintaining inhibition or repression is freed for asserting and envisaging what would otherwise be un-thinkable. But the wishful investment of the author in the hero involved a lack of distance: Marlowe *does* dare "God out of heaven *with* . . . Tamburlaine" as well as appropriate much that is heavenly. And Greene's final jibe catches the total, unre-served investment in making theatrically actual a poetry of magical expectation: the poetical spirit who sets "the end of scholarism in an English bank verse," "filling the mouth like the faburden of Bo-Bell," is "bred in Merlin's race."

In *Doctor Faustus*, the weakness got rid of in Mycetes is made part of the protagonist, as is a heroic version of the naïveté about confusing sign with significance that Marlowe

---

31. Greenblatt regards *Tamburlaine*, for instance, as "an extraordinary meditation on the roots" of contemporary behavior in the service of imperi-alistic enterprise and ideology (*Renaissance Self-Fashioning*, p. 194). Wilbur Sanders, by contrast, sees Marlowe as so locked into a battle with received opinion that he can never get beyond, except by a kind of histrionic protest, the fundamental assumptions behind the attitudes he combats: "Marlowe, unlike Shakespeare, is too close to his data, too personally entangled, yet at the same time—and perhaps because of the entanglement—detached in an artificial way" (*The Dramatist and the Received Idea: Studies in the Plays of Mar-lowe and Shakespeare* [Cambridge: Cambridge University Press, 1968], p. 241).

32. The rigorous intellectual and social irony of *The Jew of Malta* (on which Greenblatt chiefly focuses) is followed, as I see it, by the close-contained, close-lipped reckoning of *Edward II*, where motives active under the titanic denial in *Tamburlaine* are now dramatized pitilessly and pitifully in political, personal, and bodily action.

2

"The forme of Faustus fortunes good or bad"

From Bloody to Black Magic

Faustus in the opening scenes outdoes Tamburlaine in pronouncing omnipotent prospects:

> Ile be great Emprour of the world,
> And make a bridge through the moouing ayre,
> To passe the *Ocean* with a band of men,
> Ile ioyne the hils that binde the *Affricke* shore,
> And make that land continent to *Spaine,*
> And both contributory to my crowne:
> The Emprour shal not liue but by my leaue.
>
> (340–46)

But here, of course, the omnipotence is overtly *magical* and *only* expectation. The rhapsody begins, moreover, with

> Had I as many soules as there be starres,
> Ide giue them al for *Mephastophilis:*
> By him Ile be . . .
>
> (337–40)

In magic and the figure of the magus, Marlowe found a social activity outside the theater that embodied what he had earlier done with his poetry in the theater. By putting Faustus's pact with the devil inside the tragedy, he found an objective correlative for his own dependent relationship to a figure of cruel power unacknowledged in *Tamburlaine*. In dramatizing Faustus's motives for the pact and his subservience to it, he brings to bear a profound understanding, including bodily understanding, of the predicaments of Protestant theology and of tensions involved in Protestant worship, especially in the service of Holy Communion.

Despite the Christian framing, it is of course too simple to see the play as a retraction. It resituates motives active in *Tamburlaine* in a way which is irreducibly dramatic. Where *Tamburlaine* can be viewed as an unacknowledged blasphemy, *Doctor Faustus* dramatizes blasphemy. But not with the single perspective of religion: it dramatizes blasphemy also as heroic endeavor. Here again Renaissance and Reformation are both present: Protestant religious perspectives are brought to bear on, and also questioned by, magical expectation which at high moments is Promethean. Caught up to an astonishing degree in the violent cross-currents of Renaissance experience, the play tends to fall apart in paraphrase. Faustus's search for magical dominion can be turned into a fable of modern man seeking to break out of religious limitations. When one retells the story in religious terms, it tends to come out as though it were Marlowe's source, *The History of the Damnable Life and Deserved Death of Doctor John Faustus*. But by the *novum organum* of the poetic drama, Marlowe can convey experience with its own integrity, beyond categories: he can "performe, / The forme of *Faustus* fortunes good or bad" (7–8).

A combination of detachment from and involvement in both magic and religion clearly goes with this control. Marlowe was certainly no believer in literalistic or vulgar magic. "Why Madam, think ye to mocke me thus palpably?" (2 *Tam.* 3948) is Theridamas's response to Olympia's magic ointment for invulnerability. This could be Jonson's Surly in *The Alchemist*. About the learned magical expectations of the Hermetic philosophy Marlowe's complete silence is striking. Faustus as a figure of the magus commands in some ways the prestige achieved by the English Hermetic magus John Dee in the early years of Elizabeth at least, or again, precariously, by Giordano Bruno during his stay in England while Marlowe was at Cambridge. He could not have been ignorant of this tradition; his neglect of it, *as such*, fits with his rigorous university education (Bruno got short shrift at Oxford). Hermes, until the seventeenth century, was believed to have written his works in Egypt before Moses (whereas in fact they were late classical elaborations of gnostic Neoplatonism, capitalizing on the reputation of ancient Egypt for a divine wisdom—a place to go alternative to the early Christians' Palestine). For Marlowe, filtered to be sure through the informer Baines, Moses himself "was but a juggler."[1]

As Frances Yates's studies have made clear, there were students of the Hermetic books, from Ficino and Pico on down to the anonymous authors of the Rosicrucian manifestos in Germany and Robert Fludd in Jacobean England, for whom the power they promised was not clearly distinguished from science or piety. Dee's contributions to cosmography and the design of navigational instruments were substantial, though he ended his life, poverty-stricken, still trying to bring down angelic spirits by drawing the right diagrams (Jonson mocks him by the anagram DEE in the "magical" sign for Drugger's shop).[2] As for piety, Bruno put his life in the Pope's hands (and lost it at the

1. After so describing Moses, Marlowe added, at least according to Baines, "that one Heriots [Thomas Hariot] Sir W. Raleighs man Can do more than he." The Baines note is printed in Brooke, *The Life of Marlowe and the Tragedy of Dido Queen of Carthage*, pp. 98–100.

2. Frances Yates considers Jonson's well-informed, uproarious satire of Dee and company in a supplementary chapter to *Shakespeare's Last Plays: A New Approach* (London: Routledge and Kegan Paul, 1975). Her straight-faced conclusion, despite the fact that the play was written two years too early, is that "It would seem that Ben Jonson was . . . against the match [of James I's daughter Elizabeth] with the Elector Palatine" (p. 116). Both her reading of *The Alchemist* and her literalistic, politically directed readings of magical motifs in Shakespeare's late plays fail to respond to ironic distinctions between magic and imagination central to the drama—whether comic, tragic, or satiric—of the age. But the extensive, learned work Yates has done on Renaissance Hermeticism is indispensable to anyone who wishes to pursue the tradition of magic in relation to the literature of the time. The brief discussion of Hermetic magic here is particularly indebted to her great book, *Giordano Bruno and the Hermetic Tradition* (Chicago: University of Chicago Press, 1964).

stake) through conviction that he had arrived at an understanding of man's relation to God which could reconcile Christen-
dom. It was piety, however, which involved becoming, in
effect, God, according to a Neoplatonic mode of relationship
turned so as to include climbing up into deity as well as receiving divine energy streaming down.

One way to look at Marlowe's relation to the Hermetic strain
is to see the Tamburlaine plays as his bloody-minded version of
it. There is a moment in the second part when deity is described
in a way exactly consistent with Hermetic Neoplatonism:

> he that sits on high and neuer sleeps,
> Nor in one place is circumscriptible,
> But euery where fils euery Continent,
> With strange infusion of his sacred vigor.
>
> (2906–9)

In *NOUS to Hermes*, or *Corpus Hermeticum XI*, we get asser-
tions of human omnipotence of mind that parallel Faustus's expectations at the outset: "Command your soul to take itself to
India, and there, sooner than your order, it will be. Command
it to pass over the ocean, and in an instant it will be there, not
as if it had to voyage from one place to another, but as if it had
always been there. Command it to fly to heaven, it has no need
of wings: nothing can obstruct it, neither the fire of the sun, nor
the air, nor the revolution of the heavens, nor the other celes-
tial bodies."[3] We have Tamburlaine's "still climing after knowledge infinite, / And alwaies moouing as the restles Spheares,"
but his way of realizing divine potential is by rapid marches and
his conquering sword. Yet Marlowe's poetic expression of what
he achieves involves violent equivalents of the intellectual
power Nous promises Hermes: "to crack the vault of the universe itself and contemplate that which is beyond (at least if
there is anything beyond the world)."

I have quoted above one of Tamburlaine's accounts of the
identity of his own spirit with Jove's, and so his need to "leuie

---

3. This and the two following quotations from *NOUS to Hermes* are
taken from Peter J. French, *John Dee: The World of an Elizabethan Magus*
(London: Routledge and Kegan Paul, 1972), p. 75.

power against thy throne, / That I might mooue the turning Spheares of heauen" (3791–92). Nous argues that God must be conceived according to the swiftness and power that man commands. Of God, he says, "all that is, he contains within himself *like thoughts,* the world, himself, the All. If in that event you do not make yourself equal to God, you cannot know God: because like is intelligible only to like" (my italics). The Hermetic enterprise is phrased in gnostic, spiritual modes. But it could be intoxicating to the point of megalomania: Bruno especially was as self-made, self-determining, and manic as Tamburlaine, who proposes as action what Hermetic magic envisages quasi-mystically. Marlowe will not traffic in the pious imperialism of the Hermeticists; he likes his imperialism straight. But then he has an equivalent of omnipotence of *mind* by poetry in the theater.

Faustus's first description of his expectations from magic could be Hermetic:

> These Metaphisickes of Magicians,
> And Negromantike bookes are heauenly:
> Lines, circles, sceanes, letters and characters:
> I, these are those that *Faustus* most desires.
> O what a world of profit and delight,
> Of power, of honor, of omnipotence
> Is promised to the studious Artizan?
> All things that mooue betweene the quiet poles
> Shalbe at my commaund, Emperours and Kings
> Are but obeyd in their seuerall prouinces:
> Nor can they raise the winde, or rend the cloudes:
> But his dominion that exceedes in this,
> Stretcheth as farre as doth the minde of man.
> A sound Magician is a mighty god:
> Heere *Faustus* trie thy braines to gaine a deitie.
>
> (77–91)

The overt emphasis on power is emphatically secular—but similar expectations peer out from behind Hermetic gnosticism's noble and moral language. Faustus the scholar, trying on professional identities after "hauing commencde," clearly projects a version of the situation Marlowe had been in, on a scholarship intended for students planning to become divines (as his roommates did). The decision in favor of magic had an equivalent, as I have been stressing, in the decision to use poetry in the theater to write *Tamburlaine!* (And also, almost certainly, to enter the *secret* service—and know perhaps "the secrets of all forraine kings" [*Faus.* 115]).

The decision to dramatize the Faustus story, with its pact, carried with it black magic, "Negromantike," not white; it made the Christian Devil his servant, not the good demons intermediate to deity in Hermetic Neoplatonism. But Marlowe holds back the realization of this dark dependency so that Faustus can find it out for himself, in a superb dramatic double take. There is no mention of devil or pact in the opening chorus as it summarizes Faustus's career. In the opening soliloquy the "heavenly" necromantic books, with their figures, seem to be all that the studious artisan needs—with the instruction of Valdes and Cornelius. So too when they appear: "*Faustus,* / These bookes, thy wit and our experience / Shall make all nations to canonize us" (147–49). The evil angel also promises an independent dominion: "Be thou on earth as *Ioue* is in the skie, / Lord and commaunder of these Elements" (104–5). When Valdes says that "the subiects of euery element" will be "alwaies seruiceable" (151–52), they can be assumed to be spirits of white magic, such as Prospero commands in airy Ariel and earthy Caliban. It is only after the conjuring in "some lustie groue" (180) that Mephostophilis appears in a coup de theatre. He obeys Faustus's first command to disguise himself as a Friar (how on top Faustus feels with his "That holy shape becomes a diuell best" [261]). But when Mephostophilis returns, he is far from "servile"—his civilized courtesy makes him a social equal.

And it is *he,* in this very great moment of dramatic literature, who has the wit and the experience. Without realizing it, Faustus moves into the dependent position as he asks the questions and Mephostophilis gives the answers—and not the answers he expects.

> FAUSTUS: Was not that *Lucifer* an Angell once?
> MEPHOSTOPHILIS: Yes *Faustus,* and most dearely lou'd of God.
> FAUSTUS: How comes it then that he is prince of diuels?
> MEPHOSTOPHILIS: O by aspiring pride and insolence,
>   For which God threw him from the face of heauen.
>
> (300–304)

Or again, "Why, this is hel, nor am I out of it" (312). Faustus does not recognize the import of the double take as it happens: "This word damnation terrifies not him, / For he confounds hell in *Elizium*. . . ." "Learne thou of *Faustus* manly fortitude, / And scorne those ioyes thou neuer shalt possesse" (294–95, 321–22).

One can hardly admire too much the understanding Marlowe has brought to bear on the delusory side of the hopes of the Renaissance magus. (He never, so far as I am aware, did justice even by implication to the scientific side, except as it could contribute to the creation of "stranger engines for the brunt of warre" [123]. Probably he lacked the patience, in view of his need to conceive and subdue at once. And he had his own instruments and situation in the theater.) Equally stunning is the exposure, or better exposition, of the suffering sense of alienation and loss underlying the diabolic:

> Vnhappy spirits that fell with *Lucifer*,
> Conspir'd against our God with *Lucifer*,
> And are for euer damnd with *Lucifer*.
>
> . . . .
>
> Thinkst thou that I who saw the face of God,
> And tasted the eternal ioyes of heauen,
> Am not tormented with ten thousand hels,
> In being depriv'd of euerlasting blisse?
>
> (306–8, 313–16)

The repetition of "Lucifer" as the doom unfolds is on the level of Shakespeare at his best.

In the excellent comic scene which follows, Wagner with the clown is a burlesque of Faustus in his conjuring, complete with an academic servant's tags of Latin: "Ile make thee go like *Qui mihi discipulus*" (366–67). Our theatrical taste by now surely can handle the literal implausibility of his raising actual devils—and using them with a mastery already crucially disappointed in his master's conjuring. The interval gives Faustus time to begin to take in what he has learned from the devil's own mouth: "Now Faustus must thou needes be damnd, / And canst thou not be saued?" (433–34). In the next encounters, he becomes in effect "discipulus" to Mephostophilis, and a rather slow pupil at that: "and this be hell, Ile willingly be damnd here: what walking, disputing, &c." (570–71). The plot's program requires that the pact work on a narrative level, so Faustus is given magic books, taken by dragons to Rome; he can be invisible and box the pope's ear; he can have his spirits produce the royal shape of Alexander. It is hard to know how to take much of this outward action. Many critics make much of its triviality as heavily ironic. There is certainly much that lets us down, or is irrelevant—much more in the 1616 version than in the 1604.[4] The triviality is never noted as such, however, by Faustus or anybody else—even the horning of the knight and gulling of the horse courser are presented straight. Of course both texts are corrupt and include, probably even in the 1604 version, matter improvised by the acting company. It seems to me best to regret the bad text and also recognize that problems limiting what could be enacted were partly insoluble.

It is quite another matter as Mephostophilis brings Faustus up short again and again. As he refuses to provide a wife or to name God, the sense grows of Faustus being closed in on. That Faustus learns nothing now is underscored: "these slender trifles *Wagner* can decide" (661). The sweeping outreach of "Tel me, are there many heauens above the Moone?" (646)—which moves toward the plurality of worlds that Bruno asserted—is answered with a summary of the Ptolemaic universe as an en-

---

4. Almost everything I find occasion to use is in the 1604 Quarto, and I find its readings almost always superior to those of 1616. This experience, corroborated by experience with teaching *Doctor Faustus* in both versions, inclines me to regard most of the 1604 text (with some obvious interpolations) as Marlowe's, or close to Marlowe's, whereas most of the additional matter in the 1616 version seems to me to lack imaginative and stylistic relation to the core of the play. Thus my experience as a reader runs counter to the conclusions in favor of the 1616 Quarto which Greg arrives at from textual study and hypothesis in *Marlowe's "Doctor Faustus," 1604–1616: Parallel Texts.* Michael Warren, in *"Doctor Faustus: The Old Man and the Text,"* *English Literary Renaissance* 11 (1981): 111–47, has demonstrated, I think, that the 1604 and 1616 texts represent two different plays, reflecting two different developments from an original which we have no way of reconstructing from the corrupt and developed versions we have of it. Constance Brown Kuriyama, in "Dr. Greg and *Doctor Faustus*: The Supposed Originality of the 1616 Text," *English Literary Renaissance* 5 (1975): 171–97, reviews the whole body of textual criticism and provides additional evidence in presenting a closely reasoned challenge to Greg's conclusion that the 1616 version has superior authenticity.

closure: "As are the elements, such are the spheares, / Mutually folded in each others orbe" (649–50). Thomas P. Cartelli has pointed out that at one point in the Faust-book the geocentric conception is challenged, a cosmological opening up which Marlowe ignores.[5] The closing in on mind and spirit in these scenes anticipates the final enclosure, alone, in his study. And Faustus slips more and more into the propitiatory mode next door to surrender, which finally becomes "Vgly hell gape not, come not *Lucifer,* / Ile burne my bookes, ah *Mephastophilis*" (1476–77). Empson's telling observation bears repeating, that the stresses on "gape" and "come" make the line almost ask for hell and Lucifer.[6] "Loe *Mephastophilis,* for loue of thee, / I cut mine arme," (485–86) he had said as he set out. The love is never returned, except as desire "to obtaine his soule" (505). His final "ah *Mephastophilis*" still makes an appeal, even as it accepts destruction as consummation.

"to glut the longing"

The striving for endlessness and the need for an end are worked into the texture of the play with rigor and complexity that prove astonishing, as Edward Snow has shown.[7] The centrality of Faustus's insatiable longing and its radiations reflect at once the strategic historical moment when the drama was written, the strategic mastery of the author, and the desperate psychological predicament he brings to the play. My own explorations have come to center on how the longing in the work is expressed in a way that might have been satisfied by the ritual of the Holy Communion, and, more broadly, on the stresses that made Communion problematic for Protestant thought and sensibility.

Kuriyama's excellent psychological study appropriately brings into high focus a latent family constellation in which sal-

5. "Marlowe's Theater: The Limits of Possibility," Ph.D. diss., University of California, Santa Cruz, 1979, pp. 227–28.

6. William Empson, *Seven Types of Ambiguity,* rev. ed. (New York: New Directions, 1947), p. 206.

7. "Marlowe's *Doctor Faustus* and the Ends of Desire," in *Two Renaissance Mythmakers: Christopher Marlowe and Ben Jonson,* ed. Alvin Kernan, Selected Papers from the English Institute, 1975–76 (Baltimore: Johns Hopkins University Press, 1977), pp. 70–110.

vation is equivalent to an unattainable "loving and harmonious relationship with the father" and damnation means "perpetual alienation from the father's love and, on a more primitive level, the castration and death which follow as a consequence of the father's hatred."[8] But, as she herself emphasizes, the psycho-analytic perspective isolates this family-derived core from its social matrix. Each of Marlowe's plays moves out from a core of feelings grounded in family relationships and into possible modes of action, successive *theaters* of action, each different. Greenblatt emphasizes how this always moving, restless exploration of possibilities exhibits destructiveness actually in the Renaissance and Reformation world; after Tamburlaine, each successive hero self-destructs according to the pattern of the violent mode of action by which he seeks mastery.[9] In *Doctor Faustus*, the social action involves blasphemy and dependence on an alternative figure of power to God. That dependence is consummated by a black mass, alternative to Holy Communion. By performing it, Faustus seeks to serve a hunger that Communion might satisfy were it not beyond his reach.

After the opening fantasies of omnipotence, where "phallic" aggression is prominent, imagery of appetite reaching toward equivalents for Communion becomes more and more prominent. In psychoanalytic terms, this is recourse from phallic to oral modes of satisfaction and mastery, and also to a physical way of relating to worshipful figures. Such regression is explicitly central to the Communion experience of eating the body and drinking the blood of Christ; there regression can be transformed, for the successful worshiper, into reconciliation with God and community. Before we consider how this strain develops with astonishing poetic and psychological consistency in the play, it will be useful to step back and consider the tensions involved in this sacrament for the Reformation and in particular for the Elizabethan church.

Lily B. Campbell related *Doctor Faustus* to fundamental tensions in Reformation religious experience in an essay which considers Marlowe's hero, against the background of Protestant

8. *Hammer or Anvil*, p. 103.
9. *Renaissance Self-Fashioning*, pp. 193–221.

casuistry, as "a case of conscience."[10] She focuses on Faustus's
sin of despair, his inability to believe in his own salvation, a sin
to which Protestants, particularly Calvinistic Protestants, were
especially subject. They had to cope with the immense distance
of Calvin's God from the worshiper and with God's terrifying,
inclusive justice, just alike to the predestined elect and the predestined reprobate. And they had to do without much of the
intercession provided by the Roman church. Faustus's entrance
into magic is grounded in despair. He quotes crucial texts, regularly heard as part of the Anglican service:

> When all is done, Diuinitie is best.
> *Ieromes* Bible, *Faustus*, view it well.
> *Stipendium peccati mors est*: ha, *Stipendium, &c.*
> The reward of sinne is death: thats hard.
> *Si peccasse negamus, fallimur, & nulla est in nobis veritas.*
> If we say that we haue no sinne,
> We deceiue our selues, and theres no truth in vs.
> Why then belike
> We must sinne, and so consequently die.
> I, we must die an euerlasting death:
> What doctrine call you this, *Che sera, sera,*
> What wil be, shall be? Diuinitie, adieu,
> These Metaphisickes of Magicians,
> And Negromantike bookes are heauenly:
>
> (65–78)

Faustus leaves out the promises of divine grace which in the service go with "the reward of sin is death"; here, as always, he is
unable to believe in God's love for him. But he does believe,
throughout, in God's justice.

Campbell observes that it was peculiarly the God-fearing
man who was vulnerable to despair, dragged down, like Spenser's
Red Cross Knight in the Cave of Despair, by a sense of his sins.
What Despair in his cave makes Spenser's knight forget, by insisting on his sinfulness, is God's love: as Una tells him in
snatching away the dagger: "Where Justice grows, there grows

---

10. *"Doctor Faustus:* A Case of Conscience," *PMLA* 67 (1952):
219–39.

eke greater Grace." Faustus forgets this too: vivid as is his sense of the lost joys of heaven, he never once expresses any sense that God could love him in spite of his sins. "Faustus wil turne to God againe. / To God? he loues thee not" (441–42). Lucifer himself points to divine justice: "Christ cannot save thy soule, for he is iust" (697).

Campbell parallels Faustus as Marlowe presents him with the experience of Francis Spira, a historical case of conscience which became an exemplar of despair for Protestants.[11] This Italian lawyer, who in 1548 died of no outward cause, surrounded by counseling Catholic doctors but miserably certain of his own damnation, had recanted Protestant views under Catholic pressure. Earlier he had been enthusiastic in his conviction of the truth of justification by faith. In his last weeks, Spira was tormented by a burning physical sensation of thirst which no drink could assuage. Dying in terror, Spira could no longer believe in the efficacy of the Roman rites. Faustus embraces magical rituals—they are something he can *do*—though their efficacy expires with the pact, and he too dies in terror.

It is striking that Marlowe does not make a conviction of predestinate reprobation the basis for Faustus's despair, as it often was historically. Wilbur Sanders, in a discussion of the play and the Calvinist doctrine of reprobation, sees it as "a death-struggle with Calvin's God."[12] He surveys doctrinal formulations and popular tracts dealing with predestination, which he brilliantly terms "the basilisk eye of Christianity" (p. 228), to conclude that Faustus is held under its gaze "by the umbilical cord of a terror-which-is-still faith" (p. 229). Certainly he is right that the quality of Faustus's despair, his conviction that he cannot be saved, is like the anguished conviction of reprobation so many felt. But repeatedly, especially in the latter part of the play, the good angel, Faustus himself, and, most emphatically, the old man insist that grace is there. "Neuer too late, if Faustus can repent" (692).

> Ah stay good Faustus, stay thy desperate steps,
> I see an Angell houers ore thy head,

11. See ibid., pp. 225–32.
12. *The Dramatist and the Received Idea*, p. 252.

and with a violl full of precious grace,
Offers to powre the same into thy soule,
Then call for mercie and auoyd dispaire.

(1290–94)

And though these appeals sound hollow to Sanders—as they do not to me—there is the further objection that Faustus never once refers to the possibility that he is reprobate by predestination. Instead, it is what he has actively done that dooms him: "Seeing *Faustus* hath incurrd eternall death, / By desprate thoughts against *Ioues* deitie" (324–25). God's justice, not his inscrutable decision, before all time, condemns Faustus—as is appropriate as Marlowe turns from alliance with a hero who alternately defies and claims sanction from "a God full of reuenging wrath" (*2 Tamb.* 4294) to the fear and despair attending desperate thoughts against such a god.[13]

Near the end, Faustus expresses his longing for communion in imagery which reflects tensions that were involved, for the Elizabethan church, in the use and understanding of Holy Communion:

O Ile leape vp to my God: who pulles me downe?
See see where Christs blood streames in the firmament.
One drop would saue my soule, halfe a drop, ah my Christ.
Ah rend not my heart for naming of my Christ,
Yet wil I call on him: oh spare me *Lucifer!*
Where is it now? tis gone: And see where God
Stretcheth out his arme, and bends his irefull browes.

(1431–37)

The immense distance away that the blood is, streaming in the sky like the Milky Way, embodies the helplessness of the Protestant who lacks faith in his own salvation. Calvin taught that communion could come by the lifting up of the soul to heaven, that it was not necessary that the essence of the flesh descend from heaven. But Faustus must try to leap up by himself, with-

13. When one places *Doctor Faustus* thus, there is no need to think that the Calvinist doctrine *determines* its special anguish, the dramatist reacting primarily to the received idea. I find Sanders helpful on the historical context of the play's theological situation, but wrong about the play's immediate impacts, perhaps partly because he reads it in the 1616 version.

out the aid of grace. His focus on the one drop, half a drop, that he feels would save his soul, expresses the Reformation's tendency to isolate the individual in his act of communion and to conceive of his participation, as Dom Gregory Dix underscores in his great history, *The Shape of the Liturgy,* "as something *passive,* as a 'reception.'"[14] At the same time, the cosmological immensity of the imagery embodies Marlowe's characteristic sense of the vastness of the universe and, here, of the tremendousness of the God who rules it and yet concerns himself with every life, stretching out his arm and bending his ireful brows.

The piety of the late Middle Ages had dwelt on miracles where a host dripped actual blood and had depicted scenes where blood streamed down directly from Christ's wounds into the chalice on the altar. The Counter-Reformation, in its own way, pursued such physical imagery and literal conceptions, which remained viable for the Roman Catholic world as embodiments of grace. A hunger for this kind of physical resource appears in the way that Faustus envisages Christ's blood, visibly streaming, in drops to be drunk. But for the Elizabethan church, such thinking about Communion was "but to dreame a grosse carnall feeding," in the words of the homily "Of the worthy receiving of the Sacraments."[15] We have good reason to think that Marlowe had encountered Catholic ceremony during his absences from Cambridge, when the reasonable assumption is that he was working at intervals as a secret agent among Catholic English exiles and students on the Continent. The letter from the Privy Council which secured him his degree is best explained on that hypothesis, since it denies a rumor that he is "determined to have gone beyond the seas to Reames and there to remaine" (as secret Catholics were doing after graduation) and speaks of his having been employed "in matters touching

14. (London: Dacre Press, 1945), p. 635.

15. The homily was issued in the *Seconde Tome of Homelyes,* sanctioned by the Convocation of Canterbury in 1563 and "appointed to be read in all churches." It is quoted by C. W. Dugmore in *The Mass and the English Reformers* (London: Macmillan, 1958), p. 233. I am greatly indebted to Dugmore's book, and to Dix's *The Shape of the Liturgy,* throughout this discussion. Dugmore, in exploring in detail Tudor views of the real presence in the elements of the Lord's Supper and their relevant background brings into focus exactly the tensions that are relevant to *Doctor Faustus.*

the benefitt of his Countrie."[16] To have acted the part of a possible student convert would have involved understanding the Catholic point of view. And we have Marlowe the scorner's talk, again filtered through Baines, "that if there be any god or any good Religion, then it is in the papistes because the service of god is performed with more Cerimonies, as Elevation of the mass, organs, singing men, Shaven Crowns, & cta. That all protestantes are Hypocriticall asses . . ."[17]

What concerns us here is the way *Doctor Faustus* reflects the tension involved in the Protestant world's denying itself miracle in a central area of experience. Things that had seemed supernatural events, and were still felt as such in Rheims, were superstition or magic from the standpoint of the new Protestant focus on individual experience. Thus the abusive Bishop Bale calls the Roman priests' consecration of the elements "such a charm of enchantment as may not be done but by an oiled officer of the pope's generation."[18] Yet the Anglican church kept the basic physical gestures of the Mass, with a service and words of administration which leave open the question of how Christ's body and blood are consumed. And Anglican divines, though occasionally going all the way to the Zwinglian view of the service as simply a memorial, characteristically maintained a real presence, insisting, in Bishop Jewell's words, that "we feed not the people of God with bare signs and figures" (quoted ibid., p. 229). Semantic tensions were involved in this position: the whole great controversy centered on fundamental issues about the nature of signs and acts, through which the age pursued its new sense of reality.

In the church of the Elizabethan settlement, there was still, along with the Reformation's insistence that "Christ's Gospel is not a ceremonial law . . . but it is a religion to serve God, not

16. Quoted in John Bakeless, *The Tragicall History of Christopher Marlowe*, 2 vols. (Cambridge, Mass.: Harvard University Press, 1942), 1:77.

17. Brooke, *Life of Marlowe*, p. 99.

18. *Select Works of John Bale*, ed. Henry Christmas, Parker Society (Cambridge: Cambridge University Press, 1849), pp. 232–33; quoted in *The Mass and the English Reformers*, p. 235. An order in Council under Warwick in 1549 characteristically refers to "theire olde Lattenne service, their conjured bredde and water, with such lyke vayne and superstitiouse ceremonies" (quoted p. 142).

in bondage of the figure or shadow,"[19] an ingrained assumption that the crucial physical acts of worship had, or should have, independent meaning. This was supported by the doctrine of a real though not physical presence of Christ. But for many worshipers the physical elements themselves tended to keep a sacred or taboo quality in line with the old need for physical embodiment.

The Prayer Book's admonition about the abuse of Holy Communion strikingly illuminates Marlowe's dramatization of blasphemy:

> Dearly beloved in the Lord: yet that mind to come to the holy Communion of the body and blood of our Savior Christ, must consider what S. Paul writeth to the Corinthians, how he exhorteth all persons diligently to try and examine themselves, before they presume to eat of that bread, and drink of that cup: for as the benefit is great, if with a truly penitent heart and lively faith we receive that holy sacrament (for then we spiritually eat the flesh of Christ, and drink his blood, then we dwell in Christ and Christ in us, we be one with Christ, and Christ with us:) so is the danger great, if we receive the same unworthily. For then we be guilty of the body and blood of Christ our Savior. We eat and drink our own damnation not considering the Lord's body.[20]

To eat and drink damnation describes not only Faustus's attitude, but the physical embodiment of it, as we shall see in considering the ramifications of gluttony in the play.

Blasphemy implies belief of some sort, as T. S. Eliot observed in pointing, in his seminal 1918 essay, to blasphemy as crucial in Marlowe's work: blasphemy involves also, consciously or unconsciously, the magical assumption that signs can be identified with what they signify. Ministers were warned by several rubrics in the Tudor Prayer Books against allowing parishioners to convey the bread of the sacrament secretly away, lest they "abuse it to superstition and wickedness."[21] Such abuse de-

---

19. *The Two Liturgies, A. D. 1549 and A. D. 1552 . . . in the Reign of King Edward VI*, ed. Joseph Ketley, Parker Society, no. 29 (Cambridge: Cambridge University Press, 1844), p. 198.

20. *Liturgical Services . . . in the Reign of Queen Elizabeth*, ed. William K. Clay, Parker Society, no. 30 (Cambridge: Cambridge University Press, 1847), p. 189.

21. From a rubric of the first Prayer Book of Edward VI, where the

pends on believing or feeling that, regardless of its context, the
bread is God, so that by appropriating it one can magically take
advantage of God. Spelled out in this way, the magical thinking
which identifies sign and significance seems so implausible as to
be trivial. But for the sort of experience expressed in *Doctor
Faustus,* the identifications and displacements that matter take
place at the levels where desire seeks half blindly to discover or
recover its objects. Faustus repeatedly moves through a circular
pattern, from thinking of the joys of heaven, through despair-
ing of ever possessing them, to embracing magical dominion
as a blasphemous substitute. The blasphemous pleasures lead
back, by an involuntary logic, to a renewed sense of the lost
heavenly joys for which blasphemy comes to seem a hollow substitute—like a stolen Host found to be only bread after all. And
so the unsatisfied need starts his Ixion's wheel on another cycle.

The irony which attends Faustus's use of religious language
to describe magic enforces an awareness of this circular dramatic movement. "Diuinitie, adieu, / These . . . Negromantike
bookes are heauenly" (76–78). What seems to be a departure is
betrayed by "heavenly" to be also an effort to return. "Come,"
Faustus says to Valdes and Cornelius, "make me blest with your
sage conference" (126–27). And Valdes answers that their
combined skill in magic will "make all nations to canonize vs"
(149). In repeatedly using such expressions, which often "come
naturally" in the colloquial language of a Christian society,
the rebels seem to stumble uncannily upon words which con-
demn them by the logic of a situation larger than they are. So
Mephostophilis, when he wants to praise the beauty of the
courtesans whom he can give to Faustus, falls into saying:

> As wise as *Saba,* or as beautiful
> As was bright *Lucifer* before his fall.
>
> (589–90)

---

danger of such theft is made an argument against allowing the communicants
to take the bread in their own hands (*The Two Liturgies,* p. 99). The second
Prayer Book of Edward and the Prayer Book of Elizabeth stipulated that "to
take away the superstition, which any person hath, or might have in the
bread and wine, it shall suffice that the bread be such, as is usual to be eaten
at the table" and that "if any of the bread or wine remain, the Curate shall
have it to his own use" (*The Two Liturgies,* pp. 282–83; *Liturgical Services,*
p. 198).

The auditor can experience a qualm of awe in recognizing how Mephostophilis has undercut himself by this allusion to Lucifer when he was still star of the morning, bright with an altitude and innocence now lost.

The last and largest of these revolutions is the one that begins with showing Helen to the students, moves through the Old Man's effort to guide Faustus's steps "vnto the way of life" (1274), and ends with Helen. In urging the reality of grace, the old man performs the role of Spenser's Una in the Cave of Despair, but Faustus can only think "Hell calls for right" (1287). Mephostophilis, like Spenser's Despair, is ready with a dagger for suicide; Marlowe at this point is almost dramatizing Spenser. Faustus asks for "heauenly *Helen*" "To glut the longing of my hearts desire" and "extinguish cleane / Those thoughts that do disswade me from my vow" (1320–24). The speech to Helen is a wonderful poetic fusion of many elements, combining chivalric worship of a mistress with humanist intoxication over the project of recovering antiquity. In characteristic Renaissance fashion, Faustus proposes to relive classical myth in a medieval way: "I wil be *Paris* . . . weare thy colours" (1335, 1338). But these secular elements do not account for the peculiar power of the speech: the full awe and beauty of it depend on hoping to find the holy in the profane.

The prose source can provide a useful contrast here; Helen is described there so as to emphasize a forthright sexual appeal: "her hair hanged down loose as fair as the beaten Gold, and of such length that it reached down to her hams, with amorous coal-black eyes, a sweet and pleasant round face, her lips red as a Cherry, her cheeks of rose all colour, her mouth small, her neck white as the Swan, tall and slender of personage. . . . she looked round about her with a rolling Hawk's eye, a smiling and wanton countenance."[22] On the stage, of course, a full description was not necessary; but Marlowe in any case was after a different kind of meaning. He gives us nothing of the sort of enjoyment that the Faust-book describes in saying that Helen was "so beautiful and delightful a piece" that Faustus "made her his common Concubine and bed-fellow" and "could not be

---

22. *The History of the Damnable Life and Deserved Death of Doctor John Faustus* (1592), ed. William Rose (London: Routledge, n.d.), p. 179.

one hour from her, . . . and to his seeming, in time she was with child" (p. 194). There is nothing sublime about this account, but it has its own kind of strength—an easy, open-eyed relishing which implies that sensual fulfillment is possible and satisfying in its place within a larger whole. The writer of the Faust-book looked at Helen with his own eyes and his own assumption that the profane and the holy are separate. But for Marlowe—it was his great, transforming contribution to the Faust myth—magical dominion ambigiously mingles the divine and the human, giving to the temporal world a wonder and excitement appropriated, daringly and precariously, from the supernatural.

The famous lines are so familiar, out of context, as an apotheosis of love, that one needs to blink to see them as they fit into the play's motion, with the play's ironies. (Eartha Kitt, telling *Life* magazine about playing Helen opposite Orson Welles, ignored all irony, saying simply "I made him immortal with a kiss.") By contrast with the Helen of the source, who has legs, Marlowe's Helen is described only in terms of her face and lips; and her beauty is *power*:

> Was this the face that lancht a thousand shippes?
> And burnt the toplesse Towres of *Ilium*?
>
> (1328–29)

The kiss which follows is a way of reaching this source of power: it goes with a prayer, "make me immortall with a kisse," and the action is like taking Communion, promising, like Communion, a way to immortality. It leads immediately to an ecstasy, parallel to the one Tamburlaine envisaged to join Zenocrate in heaven. The soul seems to leave the body: "Her lips suckes forth my soule, see where it flies." The speech ends with a series of worshiping gestures expressing wonder, awe, and a yearning towards encountering a fatal power. It is striking that Helen comes to be compared to Jupiter, god of power, rather than to a goddess:

> O thou art fairer than the euening aire,
> Clad in the beauty of a thousand starres,
> Brighter art thou then flaming *Iupiter*,

> When he appeard to haplesse *Semele,*
> More louely then the monarke of the skie
> In wanton *Arethusaes* azurde armes,
> And none but thou shalt be my paramour.
>
> (1341–47)

Upward gestures are suggested by "the euening aire" and "the monarke of the skie"; Faustus's attitude towards Helen is linked to that of hapless Semele when Jupiter descended as a flame, and to that of the fountain nymph Arethusa when she embraced Jupiter in her spraylike, watery, and sky-reflecting arms. Consummation with the power first described in Helen's face is envisaged as dissolution in fire or water. There is no suggestion, here, that she might be an intercessor, even such as we get when Tamburlaine first describes God welcoming Zenocrate, just before he turns to resentment against her possession by amorous Jove.

I can imagine a commonsense objection at this point to the effect that after all Faustus's encounter with Helen is a sexual rhapsody, and that all this talk about it does not alter the fact: a kiss is a kiss. Mistresses, it could be added, are constantly compared to heaven and to gods, and lovers often feel, without being blasphemers, that a kiss makes mortality cease to matter. But it is just here that, at the risk of laboring the obvious, I want to insist that Marlowe's art gives the encounter meaning both as a peculiar kind of sexual experience *and* as blasphemy.

The stage directions of the 1604 text bring the old man back just at the moment when Faustus in so many words is making Helen into heaven:

> Here wil I dwel, for heauen be in these lips,
> And all is drosse that is not *Helena:*
>
> *Enter old man*
>
> (1333–34)

This figure of piety is a presence during the rest of the speech; his perspective is summarized after its close: "Accursed *Faustus,* miserable man, / That from thy soule excludst the grace of heauen" (1348–49).

Another perspective comes from the earlier scenes in the

play where the nature of heaven and the relation to it of man and
devil are established in conversations between Mephostophilis
and Faustus. For example, the large and final line before the old
man's entrance in the later scene, "And all is drosse that is not
Helena," has almost exactly the same movement as an earlier
line of Mephostophilis's which ends in "heauen":

> And to conclude, when all the world dissolues,
> And euery creature shalbe purified,
> All places shall be hell that is not heauen.
>
> (556–58)

One does not need to assume a conscious recognition by
the audience of this parallel, wonderfully ironic as it is when we
come to hear it as an echo.[23] What matters is the recurrence of
similar gestures in language about heaven and its substitutes, so
that a meaning of heaven and postures toward it are established.

The most striking element in this poetic complex is a series
of passages involving a face:

> Why this is hel, nor am I out of it:
> Thinkst thou that I who saw the face of God,
> And tasted the eternal ioyes of heauen,
> Am not tormented with ten thousand hels,
> In being depriv'd of euerlasting blisse?
>
> (312–16)

Just as Faustus's rapt look at Helen's face is followed by his kiss,
so in the lines of Mephostophilis, "saw the face of God" is followed by "tasted the eternal ioyes of heauen."

Both face and taste are of course traditional religious imagery, as is motion upward and downward. Marlowe's shaping
power composes traditional elements into a single complex gesture and imaginative situation which appears repeatedly. The
face is always high, something above to look up to, reach or
leap up to, or to be thrown down from:

---

23. The echo was first pointed out to me by James Alfred Martin, Jr., of
Union Theological Seminary.

FAUSTUS: Was not that *Lucifer* and Angell once?
MEPHOSTOPHILIS: Yes *Faustus*, and most dearely lou'd of God.
FAUSTUS: How comes it then that he is prince of diuels?
MEPHOSTOPHILIS: O by aspiring pride and insolence,
    For which God threw him from the face of heauen.

(300–304)

A leaping-up complementary to this throwing-down, with a re-lated sense of guilt, is expressed in Faustus's lines as he enters at midnight, about to conjure and eagerly hoping to have "these ioyes in full possession":

Now that the gloomy shadow of the earth,
Longing to view *Orions* drisling looke,
Leapes from th' antartike world vnto the skie,
And dimmes the welkin with her pitchy breath:
Faustus, begin thine incantations.

(235–39)

Here the reaching upward in *leaps* is dramatized by the word's position as a heavy stress at the opening of the line. There is a guilty suggestion in *gloomy*—both discontented and dark—linked with *longing to view*. An open-mouthed panting is sug-gested by *pitchy breath*, again with dark associations of guilt which carry through to Faustus's own breath as he says his *in-cantations*. The whole passage has a grotesque, contorted quality appropriate to the expression of an almost unutterable desire, at the same time that it magnificently affirms this desire by throw-ing its shadow up across the heavens.

A more benign vision appears in the preceding scene, where the magician Valdes promises Faustus that "serviceable" spirits will attend:

Sometimes like women, or vnwedded maides,
Shadowing more beautie in their ayrie browes,
Then has the white breasts of the queene of Loue.

(156–58)

Here we get an association of the breast with the face corre-sponding to the linkage elsewhere of tasting power and joy with seeing a face. The lines suggest by "ayrie browes" that the faces are high (as well as that the women are unsubstantial spirits).

The complex we have been following gets its fullest and most intense expression in a passage of Faustus's final speech, where the imagery of communion with which we began is one element. To present it in this fuller context, I quote again:

> The starres mooue stil, time runs, the clocke wil strike,
> The diuel wil come, and Faustus must be damnd.
> O Ile leape vp to my God: who pulles me downe?
> See see where Christs blood streames in the firmament.
> One drop would saue my soule, halfe a drop, ah my Christ.
> Ah rend not my heart for naming of my Christ,
> Yet wil I call on him: oh spare me *Lucifer!*
> Where is it now? tis gone: And see where God
> Stretcheth out his arme, and bends his irefull browes.
>
> (1429–37)

Here the leap is discovered to be unrealizable. Faustus's blasphemous vision of his own soul with Helen—"see where it flies"—is matched now by "See, see where Christs blood streames." It is "in the firmament," as was Orion's drizzling look. A paroxysm of choking tension at once overtakes Faustus when he actually envisages drinking Christ's blood. And yet—"one drop would saue my soule." Such communion is denied by the companion vision of the face, now dreadful, "irefull browes" instead of "ayrie browes," above and bending down in overwhelming anger, "the heauy wrath of God" (1439).

"A surffet of deadly sinne"

When we turn to consider the presentation of the underside of Faustus's motive, complementary to his exalted longings, the Prayer Book again can help us understand Marlowe. The seventeenth of the Thirty-Nine Articles contains a warning remarkably applicable to Faustus:

> As the godly consyderation of predestination, and our election in Christe, is full of sweete, pleasaunt, and vnspeakeable comfort to godly persons . . . : So, for curious and carnal persons, lacking

the spirite of Christe, to haue continually before their eyes the sentence of Gods predestination, is a most daungerous downefall, whereby the deuyll doth thrust them either into desperation, or into rechelesnesse of most vncleane liuing, no lesse perilous then desperation.[24]

Faustus is certainly a "curious and carnal person." And though he does not have "the sentence of God's predestination," as such, continually before his eyes, he has an equally devastating conviction of his own unworthiness and God's anger at him. The article relates this characteristically Calvinist predicament to the effort to use the body to escape despair: *rechelesnesse* (or *wretchlesnes*) seems to combine wretchedness and recklessness; the phrase "most vncleane liuing" suggests that the appetites become both inordinate and perverse.

The psychoanalytic understanding of the genesis of perversions can help us to understand how, as the article says, such unclean living is spiritually motivated—like blasphemy, with which it is closely associated. We have noticed how blasphemy involves a magical identification of action with meaning, of sign with significance. A similar identification appears in perversion as Freud has described it. Freud sees in perversions a continuation of the secondary sexual satisfactions dominant in childhood. The pervert, in this view, is attempting, by repeating a way of using the body in relation to a certain limited sexual object, to recover or continue in adult life the meaning of a relationship fixed on this action and object in childhood. So, for example, the sucking perversions may seek to establish a relationship of dependence by eating someone more powerful. Faustus lives for twenty-four years "in al voluptuousnesse" (328), in "rechelesnesse of most vncleane liuing": it is the meanings that he seeks in sensation that make his pleasures unclean, violations of taboo. We have seen how what he seeks from Oriòn or from Helen is an equivalent for Christ's blood, how the voluptuousness which is born of his despair is an effort to find in

---

24. Charles Hardwick, *A History of the Articles of Religion* (Cambridge: John Deighton, 1851), Appendix 3: Articles of Edward VI and Elizabeth (1552–1571), pp. 287, 289.

carnal satisfactions an incarnation. Perversion can thus be equivalent to a striving for a blasphemous communion.

In the same period that Eliot wrote the essay in which he pointed to the importance of blasphemy in Marlowe's work, his poem "Gerontion" expressed a vision of people in the modern world reduced to seeking spiritual experience in perverse sensuality and aestheticism:

> In the juvescence of the year
> Came Christ the tiger
>
> In depraved May, dogwood and chestnut, flowering judas
> To be eaten, to be divided, to be drunk
> Among whispers; by Mr. Silvero,
> With caressing hands, at Limoges
> Who walked all night in the next room;
>
> By Hakagawa, bowing among the Titians;
> By Madame de Tornquist, in the dark room
> Shifting the candles; Fraülein von Kulp
> Who turned in the hall, one hand on the door.[25]

As I read the elusive chronology of Eliot's poem, Marlowe would have envisaged Helen in the luxuriance of a "depraved May" associated with the Renaissance, from which we come down, through a characteristically telescoped syntax, to the meaner modern versions of a black mass. What immediately concerns us here is the seeking of incarnation in carnal and aesthetic satisfactions. The perverse has an element of worship in it.

When we consider the imagery in *Doctor Faustus* in psychoanalytic terms, an oral emphasis is very marked, both in the expression of longings that reach towards the sublime and in the gluttony which pervades the play and tends toward the comic, the grotesque, and the terrible. It is perhaps not fanciful to link the recurrent need to leap up which we have seen in the play's imagery with an infant's reaching upward to mother or breast, as this becomes fused in later life with desire for women as sources

---

25. *The Complete Poems and Plays: 1909–1950* (New York: Harcourt, Brace and World, 1952), pp. 21–22.

of intoxicating strength: the face as a source of power, to be obliviously kissed, "ayrie browes" linked to "the white breasts of the queene of Loue." Such imagery neighbors directly religious images, Christ's streaming blood, the taste of heavenly joys.

It is because Faustus has the same fundamentally acquisitive attitude toward both secular and religious objects that the religious joys are unreachable. The ground of the attitude that sustenance must be gained by special knowledge or an illicit bargain with an ultimately hostile power is the deep conviction that sustenance will not be given freely, that life and power must come from a being who condemns and rejects Faustus. From her psychoanalytic perspective, Kuriyama emphasizes fear of castration in *Doctor Faustus*, as in the prospect, finally realized, of being torn to pieces.[26] Certainly Lucifer is a "father substitute," an alternative to a vengeful God, who proves to be equally cruel. And the devils make phallic threats as they overawe Faustus at moments of his hesitating. But Faustus's situation is not shaped by open oedipal confrontation that runs the risk of provoking paternal rejection or retaliation. Faustus's insistent hunger for satisfaction is a more deeply regressive effort that sustains desire in the face of an unalterable rejection that has already taken place.[27] We can see Faustus's blasphemous

26. See *Hammer or Anvil*, pp. 109, 115, 124.

27. In "A Seventeenth-Century Demonological Neurosis" (*Standard Edition* 19:69–105), Freud analyzed an early eighteenth-century manuscript furnished him by a scholar who saw a resemblance to the Faust legend. This account of a miracle of the Shrine of the Virgin at Mariazell tells how in 1677 a painter, Christoph Haizmann, was released from a pact with the devil. Lacking entirely in Faustus's heroic-defiant aspirations (his torment ended when he was provided long-sought security with a place in a monastic order), Haizmann's case nonetheless furnishes some parallels to the passive underside—with its blurred sexual boundaries—of Faustus's longings. Haizmann's pact was formed when he suffered from depression following the death of his father, whose image Freud sees in the painter's conceptions of both divine and satanic beings. But Haizmann, first released from his pact by the intervention of the Virgin, endowed his devil with female breasts, which for Freud suggests a repressed "feminine attitude" toward the father as well as a displacement of "the child's tender feelings toward his mother" (19:90). Freud speculates that Haizmann "was one of those types of people who are known as 'eternal sucklings'—who cannot tear themselves away from the blissful situation at the mother's breast, and who, all through their lives, persist in a demand to be nourished by someone else" (19:104). One could

need, in psychoanalytic terms, as fixation or regression to infantile objects and attitudes, verging toward perverse developments of the infantile pursued and avoided in obscure images of sexual degradation. When the Arethusa image merges Helen with Jupiter, the longing for the taste of heavenly joys, for the breasts of Venus, moves across to suggestions of fellatio. Faustus's longing confuses or identifies the two parents, reducing each to an object to feed on, so that the need appears in fantasies of somehow eating the father, of panting for Orion's drizzling look, or, later, of desperately craving the inaccessible drop of Christ's blood. We have at such moments a shift from whole-person relationship to the search for satisfaction in "part objects" which W. R. D. Fairbairn has described.[28]

But to keep the experience in the perspective with which Marlowe's culture saw it, we must recognize that Faustus's despair and obsessive hunger go with his inability to take part in Holy Communion. In Holy Communion, he would, in the words of the Prayer Book, "spiritually eat the flesh of Christ, and drink his blood . . . dwell in Christ . . . be one with Christ." In the Lord's Supper, the very actions toward which the infantile, potentially disruptive motive tends are transformed for the successful communicant into a way of reconciliation with society and the ultimate source and sanction of society. But communion can only be reached by "a truly penitent heart" which recognizes human finitude, and with "a lively faith" in the possibility of God's love. Psychoanalytic interpretation can easily lead to the misconception that when we encounter infantile or potentially perverse imagery in a traditional culture it indicates, a priori, neurosis or degradation. Frequently, on the contrary, such imagery is enacted in ritual and used in art as a way of controlling what is potentially disruptive.[29]

Ritual is something done in common which validates the

---

wish, for our purposes, that Haizmann had been more of a person. But his weakness, so conducive to the social resolution of his conflicts, can bring out the passive, dependent side of Faustus's role, and so highlight its contrasting, abortive but heroic creativity.

28. See the papers collected in *An Object Relations Theory of Personality* (New York: Basic Books, 1954).

29. In the essay "Magical Hair," *Journal of the Royal Anthropological In-*

individual's membership in society—in the community, the Communion. Tudor rubrics instructed the minister to try to reconcile quarreling parishioners before admitting them to the Lord's Supper—as well as to seek out notorious sinners and try to bring them round to confession and reconciliation. Saint Thomas regarded the Eucharist as the most important sacrament because "the reality of the sacrament is the unity of the mystical body, without which there can be no salvation." [30] But the church as a *corpus mysticum* is never even envisaged by Marlowe's protagonist. Faustus's affinities with the individualistic trend in Protestantism come out in the loneliness of his search for equivalents for something "heauenly" to "feede my soule," passively; he does not envisage participating in a *common* sacred meal, even in the blasphemous version of the witches' coven.

Since ritual carries a social and moral meaning spontaneously understood by members of the culture, in tragedy it provides perspective on individual experience. So in *Lear* the audience feels the validity of Cordelia's appeal to the marriage service, or again, recoils at Lear's refusal to provide her with a dower. In *Doctor Faustus*, the Holy Communion has the same central significance as Faustus is swept away by currents of deep aberrant motives associated with it, motives it ordinarily serves to control. This becomes fully conscious, as such, for audience and for protagonist at the moment when Faustus seals his bargain by performing in effect a black mass—by giving his blood and testament instead of receiving Christ's. How deeply the awesome significance we have seen spelled out in the Prayer Book is built into his sensibility appears when he stabs his arm:

> My bloud conieales and I can write no more.
>
> . . . .
>
> Faustus giues to thee his soule: ah there it stayde,
> Why shouldst thou not? is not thy soule thine owne?
>
> (494, 499–500)

---

stitute 88 (pt. 2, 1958): 147–69, the anthropologist Edmund Leach has made this point in a most telling way in evaluating the psychoanalytic assumptions of the late Charles Berg in his book *The Unconscious Significance of Hair.*

30. Quoted in Sheldon S. Wolin, *Politics and Vision: Continuity and Innovation in Western Political Thought* (Boston: Little, Brown, 1960), p. 134.

This is the crucial moment, for Faustus imitates Christ in sacrificing himself—but to Satan instead of to God. A moment later he will repeat Christ's last words, "*Consummatum est.*" His flesh cringes to close the self-inflicted wound, so deeply is its meaning understood by his body.

The deep assumption that all strength must come from consuming another accounts not only for the desperate need to leap up again to the source of life, but also for the moments of reckless elation in fantasy. Faustus uses the word *fantasy* in exactly its modern psychological sense:

> . . . your words haue woon me at the last,
> To practise Magicke and concealed arts:
> Yet not your words onely, but mine owne fantasie,
> That will receiue no obiect for my head,
> But ruminates on Negromantique skill.
>
> (129–33)

Here "ruminates" carries on the imagery of gluttony. Moving restlessly around the circle of his desires, Faustus wants more from nature than nature can give, and gluttony is the form his "unclean living" characteristically takes. The verb "glut" recurs: "How am I glutted with conceit of this!" "That heauenly *Helen* . . . to glut the longing . . . " The prologue summarizes his career in the same terms,[31] introducing like an overture the theme of rising up by linking gluttony with a flight of Icarus:

> Till swolne with cunning, of a selfe conceit,
> His waxen wings did mount aboue his reach,
> And melting heauens conspirde his ouerthrow.
> For falling to a diuelish exercise,

31. I first became aware of this pattern of gluttonous imagery in teaching a cooperative course at Amherst College in 1947—before I was conscious of the blasphemous complex of taste, face, etc. The late R. A. Brower pointed to the prologue's talk of glut and surfeit as a key to the way Faustus's career is presented by imagery of eating. His remark proved an open sesame to the exploration of an "imaginative design" comparable to those he exhibits so delicately and effectively in his book, *The Fields of Light* (New York: Oxford University Press, 1951). This pattern later fell into place for me in relation to the play's expression of the blasphemous motives which I am following.

And glutted now with learnings golden gifts,
He surffets vpon cursed Negromancy.

(20–25)

On the final night, when his fellow scholars try to cheer Faustus, one of them says, "tis but a surffet, neuer feare man." He answers, "A surffet of deadly sinne that hath damnd both body and soule" (1366–68). How accurately this exchange defines the spiritual, blasphemous motivation of his hunger!

Grotesque and perverse versions of hunger appear in the comedy. Like much of Shakespeare's low comedy, the best clowning in *Doctor Faustus* spells out literally what is metaphorical in the poetry. When the comic action is a burlesque that uses imaginative associations present in the poetry, its authenticity is hard to doubt. Commentators are often very patronizing about the scene with the pope, for example; but it carries out the motive of gluttony in a delightful and appropriate way by presenting a pope "whose *summum bonum* is in bellycheare" (855) and by having Faustus snatch his meat and wine away and render his exorcism ludicrous, baffling magic with magic. Later Wagner tells of Faustus himself carousing and swilling amongst the students with "such belly-cheere, / As *Wagner* nere beheld in his Life" (1243–44). The presentation of the seven deadly sins, though of course traditional, comes back to hunger again and again, in gross and obscene forms; after the show is over, Faustus exclaims "O this feedes my soule" (781). One could go on and on.

Complementary to the active imagery of eating is imagery of being devoured. Such imagery was of course traditional, as for example in cathedral carvings of the Last Judgment and in the Hell's mouth of the stage. With being devoured goes the idea of giving blood, also traditional, but handled, like all the imagery, in a way to bring together deep implications. To give blood is for Faustus a propitiatory substitute for being devoured or torn in pieces. The relation is made explicit when, near the end, Mephostophilis threatens that if he repents, "Ile in peecemeale teare thy flesh" (1306). Faustus collapses at once into propitiation, signaled poignantly by the epithet "sweet" which is always on his hungry lips:

Sweete *Mephastophilis*, intreate thy Lord
To pardon my vniust presumption,
And with my blood againe I wil confirme
My former vow I made to *Lucifer*.
                                        (1307–10)

By his pact Faustus agrees to be devoured later provided that he
can do the devouring in the meantime. Before the signing, he
speaks of paying by using other people's blood:

The god thou seruest is thine owne appetite,
Wherein is fixt the loue of Belsabub.
To him Ile build an altare and a church,
And offer luke warme blood of new borne babes.
                                        (443–46)

But it has to be his own blood. The identification of his blood
with his soul (a very common traditional idea) is underscored
by the fact that his blood congeals as he is about to write "gives
to thee his soule," and by Mephostophilis's vampire-like ex-
clamation, as the blood clears again under the influence of his
ominous fire: "O what will not I do to obtaine his soule?" (505)
    Faustus's relation to the devil here is expressed in a way that
was characteristic of witchcraft—or perhaps one should say, of
the fantasies of witch-hunters about witchcraft. Witch lore
often embodies the assumption that power can be conveyed by
giving and taking the contents of the body, with which the soul
is identified, especially the blood. To give blood to the devil—
and to various animal familiars—was the ritual expression of
submission, for which in return one got special powers. Witches
could be detected by the "devil's mark" from which the blood
was drawn. In stabbing his arm, Faustus is making a "devil's
mark" or "witch's mark" on himself.[32]
    The clown contributes to this theme in his role as a com-

32. These notions, which are summarized in most accounts of witchcraft, are spelled out at length in M. A. Murray, *The Witch-Cult in Western
Europe* (Oxford: Oxford University Press, 1921), pp. 86–96 and *passim*. One
may have reservations as to how far what Murray describes was acted out and
how far it was fantasy, but the pattern is clear.

monsense prose foil to the heroic, poetic action of the protagonist. When Wagner buys the ragged but shrewd old "clown"
into his service, he counts on hunger:

> . . . The vilaine is bare, and out of seruice, and so hungry, that I
> know he would giue his soule to the Diuel for a shoulder of
> mutton, though it were blood rawe.
>
> (358–61)

We have just heard Faustus exclaim:

> Had I as many soules as there be starres,
> Ide giue them al for *Mephastophilis*:
>
> (338–39)

But the clown is not so gullibly willing to pay all:

> How, my soule to the Diuel for a shoulder of mutton though twere
> blood rawe? not so good friend, burladie I had neede haue it wel
> roasted, and good sawce to it, if I pay so deere.
>
> (362–65)

After making game of the sturdy old beggar's ignorance of Latin
tags, Wagner assumes the role of the all-powerful magician:

> . . . Binde your selfe presently vnto me for seauen yeeres, or Ile
> turne al the lice about thee into familiars, and they shall teare
> thee in peeces.
>
> (377–80)

But again the clown's feet are on the ground:

> Doe you heare sir? you may saue that labour, they are too familiar
> with me already, swowns they are as bolde with my flesh, as if they
> had payd for my meate and drinke.
>
> (381–84)

Mephostophilis, who is to become the hero's "familiar spirit"
(as the emperor calls him later at line 1011), "pays for" his meat
and drink, and in due course will "make bold" with his flesh.

The old fellow understands such consequences, after his fashion, as the high-flown hero does not.

One final, extraordinarily complex image of surfeit appears in the last soliloquy, when Faustus, frantic to escape from his own greedy identity, conceives of his whole body being swallowed up by a cloud and then vomited away:

> Then wil I headlong runne into the earth:
> Earth gape. O no, it wil not harbour me:
> You starres that raignd at my natiuitie,
> Whose influence hath alotted death and hel,
> Now draw vp Faustus like a foggy mist,
> Into the intrailes of yon labring cloude,
> That when you vomite foorth into the ayre,
> My limbes may issue from your smoaky mouthes,
> So that my soule may but ascend to heauen.
>
> (1441–49)

Taken by themselves, these lines might seem to present a very far-fetched imagery. In relation to the imaginative design we have been tracing, they express self-disgust in terms exactly appropriate to Faustus's earlier efforts at self-aggrandizement. The hero asks to be swallowed and disgorged, anticipating the fate his sin expects and attempting to elude damnation by separating body and soul. Yet the dreadful fact is that these lines envisage death in a way which makes it a consummation of desires expressed earlier. Thus in calling up to the "starres that raignd at my natiuitie," Faustus is still adopting a posture of helpless entreaty toward powers above. He assumes their influence to be hostile but nevertheless inescapable: he is still unable to believe in love. And he asks to be "drawn up," "like a foggy mist," as earlier the "gloomy shadow," with its "pitchy breath," sought to leap up. The whole plea is couched as an eat-or-be-eaten bargain: you may eat my body if you will save my soul.

In the second half of the soliloquy Faustus keeps returning to this effort to distinguish body and soul. As the clock finally strikes, he asks for escape in physical dissolution:

> now body turne to ayre,
> Or *Lucifer* wil beare thee quicke to hel:
> *Thunder and lightning.*

O soule, be changde into little water drops,
And fal into the *Ocean,* nere be found.

(1470–73)

It is striking that death here is envisaged in a way closely similar to the visions of sexual consummation in the Helen speech. The "body turne to ayre," with the thunder and lightning, can be related to the consummation of hapless Semele with flaming Jupiter; the soul becoming little water drops recalls the showery consummation of Arethusa. Of course the auditor need not notice these relations, which in part spring naturally from a pervasive human tendency to equate sexual release with death. The auditor does feel, however, in these sublime and terrible entreaties, that Faustus is still Faustus. Analysis brings out what we all feel—that Faustus cannot repent. Despite the fact that his attitude toward his motive has changed from exaltation to horror, he is still dominated by the same motive—body and soul are one, as he himself said in the previous scene: "hath damnd both body and soule." The final pleas themselves confirm his despair, shaped as they are by the body's desires and the assumptions those desires carry.

"as farre as doth the minde of man"

After the Marprelate controversy was handled on the stage, the prohibition of religious subject matter obviated the possibility of dealing directly and explicitly with its central act of worship. This gives a special interest to the relationships we have been tracing between religious and dramatic action. We get actions analogous to Holy Communion in Shakespeare, but they are not explicitly related to it. A striking example is in *Julius Caesar.* In Calphurnia's dream, which Shakespeare develops beyond Plutarch, Caesar's statue, "like a fountain with an hundred spouts, / Did run pure blood" (2.2.77–78), in which smiling Romans bathed their hands. Decius interprets it as a happy omen: "from you great Rome shall suck / Reviving blood," "great men shall press / For tinctures, stains, relics, and cognizance" (2.2.87–89). He and the other conspirators do indeed hope to carve up Caesar and share out his spirit among them, reviving republican Rome. After the assassination, Shakespeare makes their dipping their arms in his blood into an effort to do this, with what results the sequel shows after Antony makes the wounds speak to the mob.

Caesar concludes the scene in which his fears are overcome with "Good friends, go in, and taste some wine with me, / And we, like friends, will straightway go together" (2.2.126–27). This invitation to casual social communion wrings from Brutus the aside, "That every like is not the same, O Caesar, / The heart of Brutus earns to think upon!" (2.2.128–29). He knows that he is involved in a sacrifice, and feels anguish that it must be bloody:

> Let's be sacrificers, but not butchers, Caius.
> We all stand up against the spirit of Caesar,
> And in the spirit of men there is no blood;
> O that we then could come by Caesar's spirit,
> And not dismember Caesar! But, alas,
> Caesar must bleed for it! Ah, gentle friends,
> Let's kill him boldly, but not wrathfully;
> Let's carve him as a dish fit for the gods,
> Not hew him as carcas fit for hounds.
>
> (2.1.166–74)

Yet it is Brutus who in their staggered moment after the assassination cries out:

> Stoop, Romans, stoop,
> And let us bathe our hands in Caesar's blood
> Up to the elbows, and besmear our swords.
>
> (3.1.105–7)[33]

33. The ritual bathing of hands in Caesar's blood does not occur in Plutarch's *Lives*, either in Calphurnia's dream or in the actual assassination. "Calpurnia dreamed that she sawe . . . broken downe" a pinnacle the Senate had "set upon the toppe of Caesars house" (Geoffrey Bullough, ed., *Narrative and Dramatic Sources of Shakespeare* [London: Routledge and Kegan Paul, 1964], p. 83). In the assassination, Pompey's statue, against which the slain Caesar was driven, "ranne all of a goare bloude" (p. 86), and "Brutus and his consorts" left the Senate "having their swords bloudy in their handes" (p. 103), but the ritual use the conspirators make of Caesar's blood is Shakespeare shaping the action toward the religious mythology of his own culture.

I do not think that we need be conscious of the Christian analogies, but clearly the meaning of assassination has been shaped by Christianity. Christian interpretation can understand the play as exhibiting the need for the mystery of Christ's sacrifice leading to butchery—to use Brutus's own word. Eliot observed that Greek tragedy deals with problems whose solution had to wait for the Incarnation.[34] The relationship is there to be made for what I have come to think of as Shakespeare's post-Christian art as well as for some pre-Christian Greek art. But Shakespeare does not make it.

Marlowe's *Faustus* does make such relationship explicit—so explicit that in following out the human underside of eucharistic need in the themes of gluttony and blasphemy I have largely ignored their irreducibly dramatic combination with the heroic, "Renaissance" side of the play. Marlowe was able to present blasphemy and gluttony as he did only because he was able to envisage them also as something more or something else: "his dominion that exceedes in this, / Stretcheth as farre as doth the minde of man" (88–89). We have been considering how the play presents a shape of longing and fear which might have lost itself in the fulfillment of the Lord's Supper or become obscene and hateful in the perversions of a witches' sabbath. But in fact Faustus is neither a saint nor a witch—he is Faustus, a particular man whose particular fortunes are defined not by ritual but by drama.

When the good angel tells Faustus to "lay that damned booke aside . . . that is blasphemy" (98, 101), the evil angel can answer in terms that are not moral but heroic:

---

34. In a 1917 lecture, published, without pagination, as *Religious Drama: Medieval and Modern* (New York: House of Books, 1954), Eliot argues: "So far as the stage in general has ever been serious, it has always dealt with moral problems, with problems which in the end required a religious solution—whether this necessity was present to the mind of the author or not. This is obviously true of Greek tragedy. . . . If [Euripides's] plays are not so good as those of his two predecessors, it is because of a less profound grasp of religious and moral problems." For a discussion of how Eliot in his own drama provides Christian resolution for situations from Euripides, see C. L. Barber, "The Power of Development . . . in a Different World," in F. O. Matthiessen, *The Achievement of of T. S. Eliot,* 3d ed. (N.Y.: Oxford University Press, 1958), pp. 207, 213–42.

> Go forward *Faustus* in that famous art,
> Wherein all natures treasury is containd:
> Be thou on earth as *Ioue* is in the skie.
>
> (102–4)

It is because the alternatives are not simply good or evil that Marlowe has not written a morality play but a tragedy: there is the further, heroic alternative. In dealing with the blasphemy, I have emphasized how the vision of magic joys invests earthly things with divine attributes; but the heroic quality of the magic depends on fusing these divine suggestions with tangible values and resources of the secular world.

This ennobling fusion depends, of course, on the poetry, which brings into play an extraordinary range of contemporary life:

> From *Venice* shall they dregge huge Argoces,
> And from *America* the golden fleece,
> That yearely stuffes olde *Philips* treasury.
>
> (159–61)

Here three lines draw in sixteenth-century classical studies, exploration and commercial adventure, national rivalries, and the stimulating disruptive influence of the new supply of gold bullion. Marlowe's poetry is sublime because it extends desire so as to envisage as objects of passion the larger life of society and nature: "Was this the face that . . . "—that did what? " . . . lancht a thousand shippes?" "Clad in the beauty of . . . "—of what? " . . . a thousand starres." *Doctor Faustus* has sublime dimensions because Marlowe was able to occupy so much actual thought and life by following the form of Faustus's desire. At the same time, it is a remorselessly objective, ironic play because it dramatizes the ground of the desire which needs to ransack the world for objects; and so it expresses the precariousness of the whole enterprise along with its magnificence.

Thus Faustus's gluttonous preoccupation with satisfactions of the mouth and throat is also a delight in the power and beauty of language: "I see theres vertue in my heauenly words" (262). Physical hunger is also hunger for knowledge; his need to depend on others, and to show power by compelling others to depend on him, is also learning and teaching. Academic vices and weaknesses shadow academic virtues: there is a fine, lonely, generous mastery about Faustus when he is with his colleagues and the students; and Mephostophilis too has a moving dignity in expounding unflinchingly the dreadful logic of damnation to Faustus as to a disciple. The inordinate fascination with secrets, with what cannot be named, as Mephostophilis cannot name God, includes the exploring, inquiring attitude of "Tel me, are there many heauens aboue the Moone?" (646). The need to leap up becomes such aspirations as the plan to "make a bridge through the moouing ayre, / To passe the *Ocean* with a band of men" (341–42). Here we have in germ that sense of man's destiny as a vector moving through open space which Spengler described as the Faustian soul form. Faustus's alienation, which we have discussed chiefly as it produces a need for blasphemy, also motivates the readiness to alter and appropriate the created universe—make the moon drop or ocean rise—appropriating them for man instead of for the greater glory of God, because the heavens are "the booke of *Ioues* hie firmament" (794), and one can hope for nothing from Jove. Perhaps most fundamental of all is the assumption that power is something outside oneself, something one does not become (as a child becomes a man); something beyond and stronger than oneself (as God remains stronger than man); *and yet* something one can capture and ride—by manipulating symbols.

Marlowe of course does not anticipate the kind of manipulation of symbols which actually has, in natural science, produced this sort of power: Mephostophilis answers Faustus with Ptolemy, not Copernicus—let alone the calculus. But Marlowe was able to exemplify the creative function of controlling symbols by the way he has made poetic speech an integral part of drama as a mode of action. Faustus can assert about himself, "This word damnation terrifies not him, / For he confounds hell in *Elizium*" (294–95). The extraordinary pun in "confounds hell in Elizium" suggests that Faustus is able to change the world by the way he names it, to *destroy* or *baffle* hell by *equating* or *mixing* it with Elysium. [35]

---

35. In a commentary on the Virgilian and Averroist precedents for this

Scott Buchanan, in his discussion of tragedy in *Poetry and Mathematics*, suggested that we can see tragedy as an experiment where the protagonist tests reality by trying to live a hypothesis.[36] Elizabethan tragedy, seen in this way, can be set beside the tentatively emerging science of the period. The ritualistic assumptions of alchemy were beginning to be replaced by ideas of observation; a clear-cut conception of the experimental testing of hypothesis had not developed, but Bacon was soon to speak of putting nature on the rack to make her yield up her secrets. Faustus's scientific questions and Mephostophilis's answers are disappointing; but the hero's whole enterprise is an experiment, or "experience" as the Elizabethans would have termed it. We watch as the author puts him on the rack.

FAUSTUS: Come, I thinke hell's a fable.
MEPHOSTOPHILIS: I, thinke so still, till experience change thy minde.

(559–60)

We can see particularly clearly in *Doctor Faustus* how the new drama was a step in the developing self-consciousness of Western civilization parallel to Protestantism. The restriction of the impulse for physical embodiment in the new Protestant worship connects with a compensatory fascination with magical possibilities for self-realization and the incarnation of meaning in physical gesture and ceremony: the drama carries on, for the most part in secular terms, the preoccupation with a kind of religious meaning which had been curtailed but had not been eliminated in religion. Tamburlaine talks about himself as though from the outside, almost always to aggrandize his identity; we watch to see whether words will become deeds—whether the man will become demigod. The range of relationships expressed between self and world is much wider with Faustus: "Settle thy studies *Faustus*, and beginne . . . " (29); "what shall become of Faustus, being in hel for euer?" (1382–

---

line, in *English Studies* 41 (Dec. 1960): 365–68, Bernard Fabian argues for a sense of it consistent with my reading here.

36. (New York: John Day, 1929), pp. 183–87.

83). In the opening speech, where Faustus uses his own name seven times in trying on the selves provided by the various arts, he is looking in books for a miracle. When he finally takes up the necromantic works, there is a temporary consummation, calling for a gesture to express the new being which has been seized: "All things that mooue betweene the quiet poles / Shalbe at my commaund" (84–85). At the very end of the play, Faustus's language is still demanding miracles, while the *absence* of corroborating physical actions makes clear that the universe cannot be equated with his self: "Stand stil you euer moouing spheres of heauen" (1422).

Such centering of consciousness, providing a context for the self by naming oneself, runs through all the subsequent major drama. So of course does magical thinking. Elizabeth Sewell, in *The Orphic Muse*, observed that an original artist can make what he is doing widely comprehensible by finding a myth that embodies equivalents of the new art form.[37] Marlowe found such a myth for the Elizabethan theater in magic. The double medium of poetic drama was peculiarly effective to express the struggle for omnipotence and transcendence along with its tragic (and comic) failure. Shakespeare uses and controls the magic in the web of his art from the beginning of his career to its end. King Lear in the storm, at the summit of Elizabethan tragedy, is, like Faustus, trying, and failing, to realize magical omnipotence of mind: "All-shaking thunder, / Strike flat the thick rotundity o' th' world!" (3.2.6–7). In the next chapter I shall turn to Kyd's *Spanish Tragedy*, where outrage done to social and family piety leads the protagonist to magical thinking which is madness, and where the play ends by going out of control.

Marlowe signified *his* control in *Doctor Faustus* by writing at the end of the text, "*Terminat hora diem, Terminat Author opus.*" As my friend the late John Moore remarked, it is as though he finished the play at midnight. The final hour has terminated the work and its hero, but the author is still alive. This is another kind of power than magical dominion, a social power that depends on the resources of art realized in alliance with the "patient judgments" in an audience. Marlowe has earned an identity apart from his hero's—he is the author. In his own life,

37. (New Haven, Conn.: Yale University Press, 1960), p. 82.

what was working in the work caught up with him at Deptford.
Art, even such austere art as *Doctor Faustus,* did not save the
man in the author. But the author did save, within the limits of
art, and with art's permanence, much that was in the man, to
become part of the evolving culture in which his own place was
so precarious.

There is a limitation about *Doctor Faustus* as a tragedy,
however, that goes with its ending and the attitude expressed in
the author's postscript. The tragedy has turned into something
like—too like—a scapegoat ritual: let the hero carry off into
death the evil of the motive he has embodied, ridding it from
the author-executioner and the participating audience. The
final chorus pulls back from the hero to the relief of conventional wisdom:

> *Faustus* is gone, regard his hellish fall,
> Whose fiendful fortune may exhort the wise,
> Onely to wonder at vnlawful things,
> Whose deepenesse doth intise such forward wits,
> To practise more than heauenly power permits.
>
> (1481–85)

Beyond the limiting moral perspective of the chorus, we have
seen in detail, notably in the final soliloquy, how the fate of the
hero is integral with his motive. But it is a motive that, in its
dreadful consummation, has lost all connection with the willed
heroic alternative that gave it value as a rebellious quest for
pleasure, beauty, power.

Faustus's increasing, finally total helplessness in the grip of
his motive is part of the play's limitation. Partly this is the effect
of his egotism and alienation and the limited realization of
a social world around him. The moment of greatest human
pathos, as his end approaches, comes when he is with the
scholars:

1. SCHOLAR: Why did not Faustus tel vs of this before, that Di-
   uines might haue prayed for thee?
FAUSTUS: Oft haue I thought to haue done so, but the diuell
   threatned to teare mee in peeces, if I namde God, to fetch
   both body and soule, if I once gaue eare to diuinitie: and now
   tis too late: Gentlemen away, lest you perish with me.

2. SCHOLAR: O what shal we do to saue Faustus?
FAUSTUS: Talke not of me, but saue your selues, and depart.
3. SCHOLAR: God wil strengthen me, I wil stay with Faustus.
1. SCHOLAR: Tempt not God, sweete friend, but let vs into the
   next roome, and there pray for him.
FAUSTUS: I, pray for me, pray for me, and what noyse soeuer yee
   heare, come not vnto me, for nothing can rescue me.
2. SCHOLAR: Pray thou, and we will pray that God may haue
   mercy vpon thee.
FAUSTUS: Gentlemen farewel, if I liue til morning, Ile visite you:
   if not, Faustus is gone to hel.
ALL: Faustus, farewel.

Exeunt Scholars
(1400–18)

Here, in some of the most effective writing in the play, is the only moment when Faustus feels the loss not of his own soul, or of heaven for his soul, but of human society: "Ah my sweete chamber-fellow! had I liued with thee, then had I liued stil, but now I die eternally . . . " (1359–60). But it is pathetic rather than tragic: the loss Faustus expresses is for a kind of fulfillment that he has neither sought nor left behind in his heroic enter-prise. Compare, by contrast, Macbeth's stark realization that "honor, love, obedience, troops of friends, / I must not look to have" (5.3.25–26), which becomes fully tragic through its rela-tion to the fulfillment he has known and lost in the social world he disrupts.

More full-hearted tragedy presents a protagonist committed to his heroic motive, on terms that he establishes, right through to the end—which in a tragic situation is his end. Bruno in Rome, recanting his recantation, becomes a tragic figure. Coriolanus, in his quest for heroic martial identity, is almost as self-isolating as Faustus, and Shakespeare's play presents him nearly as clinically as Marlowe's does Faustus. But Coriolanus never surrenders the heroic dimension of the motive that has animated his quest, even though Shakespeare ruthlessly drama-tizes the self-destructiveness at its psychological core. When, after his mother has persuaded him to spare Rome, Coriolanus is back at Corioli, Aufidius's accusation rests on a shrewd in-sight into the protagonist's withdrawal: "at his nurse's tears / He whin'd and roar'd away your victory" (5.6.96–97). To

Coriolanus's outraged "Hear'st thou, Mars?" Aufidius cunningly
answers: "Name not the god, thou boy of tears!" (5.6.99–100).
The hero's response is to reassert his driving motive to escape
"boy" by martial prowess.

> Measureless liar, thou hast made my heart
> Too great for what contains it. "Boy"? O slave!
> . . . .
> Cut me to pieces, Volsces, men and lads,
> Stain all your edges on me. "Boy," false hound!
> If you have writ your annals true, 'tis there
> That, like an eagle in a dove-coat, I
> Flutter'd your Volscians in Corioles.
> Alone I did it. "Boy"!
>
> (5.6.102–3; 111–16)

He would rather mean than be—mean what he has made
the name Coriolanus mean—even in the impossible situation
among Volscians to which his motive has brought him.

At the very end of *Coriolanus* there is a tribute to the protagonist's human achievement. Second Lord tries to intervene
in the assassination:

> Peace ho! no outrage, peace!
> The man is noble, and his fame folds in
> This orb o' th' earth. His last offenses
> Shall have judicious hearing.
>
> (5.6.123–26)

The conspirators cut him down nevertheless, and Aufidius
"*stands on him,*" fulfilling *his* motive. But Shakespeare concludes the play with a change of heart, even in Aufidius:

> My rage is gone,
> And I am struck with sorrow. Take him up.
> Help, three a' th' chiefest soldiers; I'll be one.
> Beat thou the drum, that it speak mournfully,
> Trail your steel pikes. Though in this city he
> Hath widowed and unchilded many a one,
> Which to this hour bewail the injury,
> Yet he shall have a noble memory.
>
> (5.6.146–53)

In *Doctor Faustus,* by contrast, the failure of the final choric judgment to locate the protagonist's heroic significance in a larger human context reflects Faustus's withdrawal from his own endeavor. With Faustus we miss, after the opening scene, heroic commitment to the motive at the base of his identity. Instead we are shown his frantic efforts to escape identity.

There is a devastated feeling at the close of *Doctor Faustus,* in my experience almost shattering. None of the strange feeling *for* life comes through at the end, such as we get in Shakespeare (though perhaps less in *Coriolanus* than in any other major tragedy). Snow has suggested that the center of feeling in *Doctor Faustus* is somehow outside the central conflict, displaced by the gap that opens between "the phenomenological contours of the play" and Faustus's consciousness.[38] Perhaps one can say that it moves more and more away from the protagonist as his helplessness and the play's understanding of it increase. *Tamburlaine* is limited by Marlowe's identification with a protagonist who himself dominates others by "conceiving and subduing both." In the more complex action of *Doctor Faustus,* identification gives way to the ever-widening distance the author puts between himself and what in him animates his protagonist. As Marlowe's Latin postscript boasts, it is another instance of "conceiving and subduing both."

38. "Marlowe's *Doctor Faustus* and the Ends of Desire," p. 73.

3

Unbroken Passion: Social Piety and Outrage in *The Spanish Tragedy*

He that will swear, that *Ieronimo,* or *Andronicus* are the best plays, yet, shall pass unexcepted at, here, as a man whose judgement shows it is constant, and hath stood still, these five and twenty, or thirty years.

Jonson, Induction to *Bartholomew Fair* (1614)

. . . those so bitter times and priuie broken passions . . .

Kyd's dedication of his translation of *Cornelia* to the Countess of Sussex

If only Kyd's language were more consistently effective, *The Spanish Tragedy* might still have a regular place in our historical repertory; its theatrical design, repeatedly apposite for Shakespeare, is nothing less than great, strategically great. In moments of immediate dramatic interplay, Kyd's dialogue is often splendidly tough and rapid, and not infrequently beautifully ironic. The formal style of his set speeches, with their elaboration of antitheses, symmetrical and cumulative patterning, and sententious apothegms, sometimes is very effective, as instances to follow will show. At its best, this formal style is "an honest method, as wholesome as sweet, and by very much more handsome than fine," to quote Hamlet's nostalgic praise for the

older drama which Shakespeare imitated for his play-within-
the-play; but often there is "matter in the phrase that might in-
dict the author of affection," especially in Kyd's use of Latin tags
(*Ham.* 2.2.442–45). The sad fact is that Kyd again and again
runs on too long to fill out a pattern: he will reduplicate and
amplify far beyond the point of diminishing returns, say what
could go without saying, and too often say it indifferently or
downright badly. In pulling out the quotations from his text
that follow in this chapter, I have constantly had to cut super-
fluous or ungainly lines; even so, his way of elaborating system-
atically has forced me to quote at greater length than is usually
necessary. Since few of us are as familiar with Kyd's play as we
are with Shakespeare's work or Marlowe's, to present key places
in it seems necessary, even if his prolixity makes doing so cum-
bersome. The tantalizing thing is that when he is good, he is
very, very good. I have often had to resist the temptation to
interrupt my argument to praise fine things which suddenly
happen in the midst of pedestrian stretches. Andrea's prologue
is chugging along through its Senecan travelogue, for instance,
when suddenly the verse rises to a line like "Pluto was pleas'd
and seal'd it with a kiss"—a kind of paradigm of Elizabethan
blank verse at its golden moment.

The Social Drama

The social and family piety so consistently absent in Marlowe's
works animates Kyd's revenge play, where outrage to the
moral order is suffered rather than initiated by the protagonist
Hieronimo. The murder of his son Horatio prevents the transmission of heritage from generation to generation and is felt to
destroy the basis of the hero's identity. The result is that the
initial general allegiance to society is called in, so to speak, and
reinvested in a new, obsessive piety centered in the lost child.
Desperate remonstrance and complaint express shocked disillu-
sion and alienation. The situation of the outraged hero seeking
vindication is expressed by poetry of magical expectation putting pressure on action, but in frustration rather than mimed
triumph of omnipotence of mind. Distraction or madness presses
toward making word become deed, or do for deed, in spite of
often absurd contradiction by the facts as manifest to bystanders

and the audience. This language of heroic adversity, in wresting words and things to its need, can become aggressive wit: outrageous antic behavior finds release in moments of delusion. The outer world goes its accustomed way, resisting the hero's need and isolating him. The need to act out, leading at first to passionate protest and then to crazy behavior, is fulfilled in the end by turning acting into action—by murdering the murderers as they perform in a play-within-the-play.

The kind of drama Kyd pioneered here proved congenial to Shakespeare. His first tragedy, *Titus Andronicus,* is a play of social piety, outrage, suffering, and revenge in Kyd's mode, and *Hamlet* is another. While we do not have the original version of *Hamlet* which Kyd almost certainly wrote, we do have *The Spanish Tragedy.* It is easy to caricature it by focusing on its "Senecan" machinery and violence in isolation from the very carefully built social situation in which they erupt. But to recognize the deep civic feeling that shapes the play and that fuels the sense of outrage on which it centers, it is crucial to understand its social dynamics. Kyd's play expresses, in the process of dramatizing outrage, the optimistic public Tudor social pieties with which Shakespeare began. In it we can see the potentially disruptive relation of the drama to this heritage.

The political and social processes which lead to the murder of Horatio are very clearly worked out. He is getting in the way of a dynastic marriage. He is put out of the way by the childless Spanish king's nephew, Lorenzo, and the crown prince of Portugal, Balthazar, because the liaison Horatio is entering into with Lorenzo's sister Bel-imperia would prevent her marrying the crown prince. The play begins after the defeat of Portugal in a battle in which Bel-imperia's first lover Andrea (also a knight below her royal caste) has been unchivalrously killed by Balthazar and his halberdiers. Balthazar was in turn overcome in a single combat and forced to surrender by Horatio, ambiguously seconded by Lorenzo, who disputes the honor of the capture with the real victor. Lorenzo is an actively ruthless Machiavel, expert in "policy" and like "to wear the crown of Spain" (fifth add., 35). The captured Portuguese prince is complacently cooperative, both in the murder and in wooing Bel-imperia in the best poetical fashion before and after it. Bel-imperia, sequestered from the court by her brother after the murder, regains her freedom of action by pretending to accept her brother's explanation that he did what he did to save her honor, and seems to acquiesce in the dynastic marriage. Secretly, she allies herself with Hieronimo, and they take vengeance by means of the play-within-the-play, staged as part of the wedding celebration.

The murder of Horatio reflects the kind of thing that could actually happen: one can recall Leicester's wife's "accident" when she fell down stairs and broke her neck, conveniently freeing Elizabeth's favorite to try to marry her. The incongruity between ruthless maneuver and the ideal social norm is built into *The Spanish Tragedy* by the contrast between the younger members of the Spanish and Portuguese royal houses and the fine, upright, well-meaning king of Spain, with his brother Castile, and their trusted official Hieronimo. The murder is (rather implausibly) kept secret from the king, and he and his brother remain solicitous about Hieronimo in his distraction. For them, the dynastic marriage is legitimate, constructive state business, and they are concerned, but blandly confident, that Bel-imperia's feelings be brought round. The deliberate, long-winded scenes of state business, which get the play off to a slow start, have the important function of exhibiting a valid social order in Spain, where the gracious king does scrupulous justice and commands the full loyalty of Hieronimo and his son:

> But now Knight Marshal, frolic with thy king,
> For 'tis thy son that wins this battle's prize.
> HIERONIMO: Long may he live to serve my sovereign liege,
> And soon decay unless he serve my liege.
>
> (1.2.96–99)

In Portugal there is a mirroring action, also slow-moving, where injustice is almost done when the distraught viceroy (or king) receives an erroneous report of his son Balthazar's death in the defeat by Spain. He is persuaded by an "envious forged tale" in which a devious courtier charges that a rival he wishes to do in has shot Prince Balthazar in the back. Just after we see Horatio murdered, the scene shifts back to Portugal and the righting of this wrong as the news arrives that Balthazar is alive in honorable captivity, with a marriage in prospect that will reconcile Portugal with Spain. The punishment of the villain— whose treachery is discovered just in time to prevent the burning alive of his slandered rival—provides an exemplum of public justice working and state business going forward, in immediate juxtaposition with the helplessness Hieronimo experiences.

By dramatizing the political order working to secure justice through the integrity of those who preside over it, Kyd grounds his action in assumptions about the social order wholly alien to Marlowe but essential to the ways in which Shakespeare will come to use tragedy. *The Spanish Tragedy* begins with an embodiment of the high-minded social and political ideal that Claudius will try to fabricate to cover his crime at the outset of *Hamlet*. For the prince, that ideal has been buried with his royal father; Hamlet will begin in a situation of desperation such as Hieronimo will come to find himself in with the murder of his son. In *Hamlet*, however, as in *The Spanish Tragedy*, the outrageous violation of the social ideal by the destruction of a family bond essential to the protagonist's sense of himself, together with insurmountable obstacles that frustrate its recovery, will lie at the heart of an action that will bring down an entire ruling order. But where Hamlet is the king's son, and "likely, had he been put on, / To have prov'd most royal" (5.2.397–98), Kyd locates his protagonist in a social situation attendant to royalty.

Hieronimo has a very clearly defined social position that makes him an appropriate figure for a middle-class London audience to identify with. He is not a member of the high nobility but a high civil servant, a former advocate who has the confidence and affection of the king in performing the office of knight marshal. The knight marshal was charged in the English court with maintaining the peace within twelve miles of the royal presence. We see Hieronimo exercising his function. Poor petitioners come to ask him to plead for them, because

> for learning and for law,
> There's not any advocate in Spain
> That can prevail, or will take half the pain
> That he will, in pursuit of equity.
>
> (3.13.51–54)

He is the type of the royal civil servants in Elizabeth's court who won their way to favor and founded important families, men of high morale and education, formed by humanist ideals. This is the sort of man Kyd would look up to, himself the son of a scrivener, and a client of a noble family who respected learning. Hieronimo can furnish a play for the wedding because

> When I was young, I gave my mind
> And plied myself to fruitless poetry:
> Which though it profit the professor naught,
> Yet is it passing pleasing to the world.
> . . . .
> When in Toledo there I studied,
> It was my chance to write a tragedy.
>
> (4.1.71–74,77–78)

The author of the additions to the Quarto of 1602 caught the likeness of Hieronimo to this type of Elizabethan worthy. He asks a painter, whose son was also murdered, to paint a family picture of him with his wife and his lost son, the sort of portrait we can still see in some Tudor houses:

> PAINTER: Sir, I am sure you have heard of my painting, my name's Bazardo.
> HIERONIMO: Bazardo! afore God, an excellent fellow! Look you sir, do you see, I'd have you paint me in my gallery, in your oil colours matted, and draw me five years younger than I am—do you see, sir, let five years go, let them go like the marshal of Spain—my wife Isabella standing by me, with a speaking look to my son Horatio, which should intend to this or some such like purpose: 'God bless thee, my sweet son,' and my hand leaning upon his head, thus sir, do you see? May it be done?
> PAINTER: Very well, sir.
> HIERONIMO: Nay, I pray mark me, sir. Then sir, would I have you paint me this tree, this very tree. Canst paint a doleful cry?
> PAINTER: Seemingly, sir.
> HIERONIMO: Nay, it should cry: but all is one. Well sir, paint me a youth, run through and through with villains' swords, hanging upon this tree. Canst thou draw a murderer?
>
> (fourth add.,115–33)

The portrait embodies the expectation of founding a "line" which was destroyed in the outrageous moment to which Hieronimo obsessively returns: "So should the lines of life that life repair . . . "[1]

Horatio, as the able son of such an official, is a rising man, such as the old nobility often resented—witness the tennis court episode when the Earl of Oxford insultingly claimed precedence over Sir Philip Sidney, the son of just such an official as Hieronimo. The caste difference is kept constantly in view from the first appearance of the young men, who dispute the honor of capturing Balthazar, and the ransom. It is even apparent in the pronouns Prince Balthazar uses in acknowledging that he yielded "To him [Lorenzo] in courtesy, to this [Horatio] perforce: / He spake me fair, this other gave me strokes . . ." (1.2.161–62)— "this" and "this other" place Horatio at a distance. The king's award is admirably judicious:

> Nephew, thou took'st his weapon and his horse,
> His weapons and his horse are thy reward.
> Horatio, thou didst force him first to yield,
> His ransom therefore is thy valour's fee:
>
> . . . .
>
> But nephew, thou shalt have the prince in guard,
> For thine estate best fitteth such a guest:
> Horatio's house were small for all his train.
>
> (1.2.180–83,185–87)

At the subsequent banquet in honor of the victory, the king places Horatio socially in placing his guests—in a manner which accepts as a matter of course the gulf of caste difference:

> Sit down young prince, you are our second guest:
> Brother sit down, and nephew take your place:
> Signior Horatio, wait thou upon our cup,
> For well thou hast deserved to be honour'd.
>
> (1.4.128–31)

1. Shakespeare, Sonnet 16.

The matter of the ransom comes up, after Horatio's murder, in the great scene of protest in which Hieronimo tries to interrupt state business but is kept back by Lorenzo. The Portuguese ambassador reports that the king his master is overjoyed by the proposed marriage and will come himself to see it solemnized, to knit an "everlasting league" with Spain, "give his crown to Balthazar, / And make a queen of Bel-imperia" (3.12.47–50).

> AMBASSADOR: Now last, dread lord, here hath his highness sent
> (Although he send not that his son return)
> His ransom due to Don Horatio.
> HIERONIMO: Horatio? who calls Horatio?
> KING: And well remember'd, thank his majesty.
> Here, see it given to Horatio.
> HIERONIMO: Justice, O justice, justice, gentle king!
> KING: Who is that? Hieronimo?
> HIERONIMO: Justice, O justice! O my son, my son,
> My son, whom naught can ransom or redeem!
> LORENZO: Hieronimo, you are not well-advis'd.
> HIERONIMO: Away Lorenzo, hinder me no more,
> For thou hast made me bankrupt of my bliss.
> Give me my son! You shall not ransom him.
> Away! I'll rip the bowels of the earth,
> *He diggeth with his dagger.*
> And ferry over to th'Elysian plains,
> And bring my son to show his deadly wounds.
> Stand from about me!
> I'll make a pickaxe of my poniard,
> And here surrender up my marshalship:
> For I'll go marshal up the fiends in hell,
> To be avenged on you all for this.
> KING: What means this outrage?
> Will none of you restrain his fury?
> HIERONIMO: Nay, soft and fair: you shall not need to strive,
> Needs must he go that the devils drive.   *Exit.*
> KING: What accident hath happ'd Hieronimo?
> I have not seen him to demean him so.
> LORENZO: My gracious lord, he is with extreme pride,
> Conceiv'd of young Horatio his son,
> And covetous of having to himself
> The ransom of the young prince Balthazar,
> Distract, and in a manner lunatic.

KING: Believe me, nephew, we are sorry for't:
    This is the love that fathers bear their sons:
    But gentle brother, go give to him this gold,
    The prince's ransom: let him have his due,
    For what he hath Horatio shall not want:
    Haply Hieronimo hath need thereof.
LORENZO: But if he be thus helplessly distract,
    'Tis requisite his office be resign'd,
    And given to one of more discretion.
KING: We shall increase his melancholy so.
    'Tis best that we see further in it first.

(3.12.57–100)

I quote at such length because the effect of Hieronimo's famous "outrage"—as the king calls it—depends on the context of ongoing, coherent state business, including the rewarding of the loyal service of which Hieronimo was so proud and about which the king is so scrupulous. The observation that the gold can be given to Hieronimo, who may need it, "For what he hath Horatio shall not want," shows that the king is thinking of the two of them as a "house"; the ransom is the kind of reward which could make a substantial difference in their fortunes. But the outrage done Hieronimo has destroyed the possibility of the system's working: "My son, whom naught can ransom or redeem!"

The affair Bel-imperia initiates with Horatio is obviously extremely dangerous. Kyd handles their liaison with great skill so as to express at one and the same time the menace it is subject to and the positive energies of life which flow into it. Bel-imperia's strange quasi-allegorical name (like a name in *The Faerie Queene*) suggests ruling power that is beautiful, fitting well with the dynastic theme. In her feminine way, she is as direct in pursuing her desires as her brother, and she shares with him the aristocratic assumption that she shall have what she wants. She had already taken a lover of lower station in Andrea. Now, in response to Horatio, she asks herself, "How can love find harbour in my breast, / Till I revenge the death of my beloved?" and answers with "Yes, second love shall further my revenge. / I'll love Horatio, my Andrea's friend, / The more to spite the prince that wrought his end" (1.4.64–68). When

139

Lorenzo exacts his sister's secret from Pedringano, his surprise is expressed by reference to Horatio's status:

> PEDRINGANO: If Madam Bel-imperia be in love—
> LORENZO: What, Villain, ifs and ands?   [*Offer to kill him.*]
> PEDRINGANO: O stay my lord, she loves Horatio.
>   BALTHAZAR *starts back.*
> LORENZO: What, Don Horatio our Knight Marshal's son?
>   (2.1.76–79).

Kyd is presenting the sort of situation Webster develops when the Duchess of Malfi marries her steward and incurs her brothers' savage reaction. The scene in which Lorenzo and Balthazar, from a hidden vantage, overlook the lovers' avowals and make antiphonal comments is a splendid use of the dimensions of the stage to space out different levels of consciousness and so convey both love-directed and death-directed energies:

> BEL-IMPERIA: But whereon dost thou chiefly meditate?
> HORATIO: On dangers past, and pleasures to ensue.
> BALTHAZAR: On pleasures past, and dangers to ensue.
> BEL-IMPERIA: What dangers and what pleasures dost thou mean?
> HORATIO: Dangers of war, and pleasures of our love.
> LORENZO: Dangers of death, but pleasures none at all.
> BEL-IMPERIA: Let dangers go, thy war shall be with me,
> But such a war, as breaks no bonds of peace.
>   .   .   .   .
> HORATIO: But gracious madam, then appoint the field
> Where trial of this war shall first be made.
> BALTHAZAR: Ambitious villain, how his boldness grows!
> BEL-IMPERIA: Then be thy father's pleasant bower the field.
>   (2.2.26–33,39–42)

It is striking that nowhere in the play is there comment or condemnation of the liaison as immoral: her brother justifies his action as done "to save your honour and mine own . . . remembering that old disgrace / Which you for Don Andrea had endur'd" and which would have been renewed had she been "found so meanly accompanied" (3.10.38,54–55,57).

Kyd is probably mirroring the actual sexual mores of more than a few aristocrats, without the theater's usual moral coloration. He also has a compositional reason for not discrediting the relation with Horatio, for the positive, life-oriented power in it is taken up into Hieronimo's protest and Bel-imperia's alliance with him. That energy is in the continued love-war metaphor, which effectively expresses the expectation of sexual death just before real death breaks in:

> BEL-IMPERIA: Nay then, to gain the glory of the field,
>   My twining arms shall yoke and make thee yield.
> HORATIO: Nay then, my arms are large and strong withal:
>   Thus elms by vines are compass'd till they fall.
> BEL-IMPERIA: O let me go, for in my troubled eyes
>   Now may'st thou read that life in passion dies.
> HORATIO: O stay awhile and I will die with thee,
>   So shalt thou yield and yet have conquer'd me.
> BEL-IMPERIA: Who's there? Pedringano! We are betray'd!
>   *Enter* LORENZO, BALTHAZAR, SERBERINE, PEDRINGANO,
>   *disguised.*
> LORENZO: My lord, away with her, take her aside.
>   O sir, forbear, your valour is already tried.
>   Quickly despatch, my masters.   *They hang him in the arbour.*
> HORATIO: What, will you murder me?
> LORENZO: Ay, thus, and thus, these are the fruits of love.
>   *They stab him.*
> BEL-IMPERIA: O save his life and let me die for him!
>   O save him brother, save him Balthazar:
>   I lov'd Horatio but he lov'd not me.
> BALTHAZAR: But Balthazar loves Bel-imperia.
> LORENZO: Although his life were still ambitious proud,
>   Yet is he at the highest now he is dead.
> BEL-IMPERIA: Murder! murder! Help, Hieronimo, help!
> LORENZO: Come stop her mouth, away with her.
>   *Exeunt, leaving Horatio's body.*
>   [2.5]
>   *Enter* HIERONIMO *in his shirt, & c.*
> HIERONIMO: What   outcries   pluck   me   from   my   naked
>   bed, . . .
>
>   (2.4.42–64, 2.5.1)

The flow of an outgoing erotic and social energy is suddenly stopped. The risk of sexual outgoing is in the military imagery, which also reminds us of Horatio's going out earlier into the world of battle. Lorenzo's "O sir, forbear, your valour is already tried," addressed as I think to Horatio as he tries to reach for his sword,[2] is a brutal mock which frustrates the expectations of chivalry. The cruel satisfaction of Lorenzo's caste feeling against rising men is in his final mock:

> Although his life were still ambitious proud,
> Yet is he at the highest now he is dead.

"Religious" Outrage

I have postponed considering the Senecan figures of the ghost of Andrea and his companion Revenge and have concentrated on the daylight world Kyd so firmly and complexly presents, because to think of him as creating a Senecan tragedy is extremely misleading. What he presents is a Senecan mood and logic of violence breaking out in a world of positive social values of graciousness, loyalty, heroism, familial love, and romantic love. Senecan mythological machinery and tags of Latin verse borrowed or imitated from Seneca and other Roman writers, beyond just being picturesque and respectably sententious, have serious meaning for Kyd: they sanction or embody the idea that there are human situations in which it can become an irrepressible necessity to return violence for violence. Seneca's own plays present a universe where this idea is pervasive, but in which the possibility of a sanctified, legitimate social order, to which men of integrity are internally related, is not important. A moral response, in Seneca's period of social disintegration, is achievable only at the very limits of horror, by arousing in his reader a shiver of awe which reanimates a still surviving taboo as his protagonists violate it. I have a sense of his pushing as far as he can for outrageousness which can still shock; in some ways he is "our contemporary." But Seneca was not Kyd's contemporary, nor Shakespeare's, *pace* Jan Kott, because their sensibility

---

2. Arthur Freeman reads it as addressed to Balthazar, which would be distracting in such rapid action, and out of place as a rude reminder of Balthazar's failure in battle. See *Thomas Kyd: Facts and Problems* (Oxford: Clarendon Press, 1967), p. 88.

is grounded in expectations of a sanctified social world, and their tragedy involves loss shaped by this expectation.

The expectation produces the special quality of shocked incredulity with which outrage is experienced by Kyd's injured hero and gives a wider justification to his being outrageous in return.[3]

> O sacred heavens! if this unhallow'd deed,
> If this inhuman and barbarous attempt,
> If this incomparable murder thus
> Of mine, but now no more my son,
> Shall unreveal'd and unrevenged pass,
> How shall we term your dealings to be just,
> If you unjustly deal with those that in your justice trust?
>
> (3.2.5–11)

The same thing is true, in a more complex way, in *Hamlet*: the intensity of the prince's anguished need for vengeance is a function of the violation of an original investment of social piety. Hamlet's piety was grounded in the figure of the father as "so excellent a king," the vital center of a heroic society, and the partner in a sacred royal marriage. Because of violated social sanctity, of broken heritage, vengeance is potential vindication, restoration. This dimension in part explains, I think, why the revenge play could become such an important form.

The fact that Kyd is dramatizing not a Senecan world but a good world becoming Senecan accounts for the curiously static and detached quality of the induction and subsequent choruses. The ghost of Andrea and Revenge are the representatives of a

---

3. The word "outrage" is used repeatedly: in the root sense, from "ultra," of going beyond bounds, as in the king's response to Hieronimo's desperate plea: "What means this outrage? / Will none of you restrain his fury?" (3.12.79–80) or Bel-imperia's "What means this outrage that is offer'd me? / Why am I thus sequester'd . . . ?" (3.9.1–2); in the sense of a disrupting response, as by Isabella's maid when "*she runs lunatic*": "Good madam, affright not thus yourself / With outrage for your son" (3.8.7–8); and in the sense, by association with the verb "rage," of raging out, by Isabella after the discovery of her dead son: "Blow, sighs, and raise an everlasting storm: / For outrage fits our cursed wretchedness" (2.5.44–45).

Senecan underworld from which they have come to watch its logic of vengeance assert itself in the upper world. Andrea's eighty-five-line opening is a measured account, very literary, in the manner of the metrical tragedies:

> In secret I possess'd a worthy dame,
> Which hight sweet Bel-imperia by name.
>
> . . . .
>
> When I was slain, my soul descended straight
> To pass the flowing stream of Acheron . . .
>
> (1.1.10–11, 18–19)

—and so to a sixty-five-line Virgilian sight-seeing trip, past the standard sights, Acheron, Cerberus, Minos, Aeacus, Rhadamanth, Hector, Achilles, Ixion, and on to Pluto's court, where

> I show'd my passport humbled on my knee:
> Whereat fair Proserpine began to smile,
> And begg'd that only she might give my doom.
> Pluto was pleas'd and seal'd it with a kiss.
> Forthwith, Revenge, she rounded thee in th'ear.
>
> . . . .
>
> REVENGE: Then know, Andrea, that thou art arriv'd
> Where thou shalt see the author of thy death,
> Don Balthazar the prince of Portingale,
> Depriv'd of life by Bel-imperia:
> Here sit we down to see the mystery,
> And serve for Chorus in this tragedy.
>
> (1.1.77–81, 86–91)

Andrea is in a curious way a kind of double of Horatio before the fact, another fine young man of moderate birth and high but precarious achievement. As Bel-imperia's former lover and Horatio's friend, Andrea becomes in effect a rooter for vengeance on the side lines, and an amusingly naive one at that. His companion spectator, Revenge, has to keep putting him right about the ironic workings of "the mystery, . . . this tragedy." At the end of act 1 Andrea exclaims

> Come we for this from depth of underground,
> To see him feast that gave me my death's wound?
>
> . . . .
>
> Nothing but league, and love, and banqueting!

REVENGE: Be still, Andrea, ere we go from hence,
    I'll turn their friendship into fell despite,
    Their love to mortal hate.

                           (1.5.1–2, 4–7)

At the end of act 2:

    Brought'st thou me hither to increase my pain?
    I look'd that Balthazar should have been slain:
    But 'tis my friend Horatio that is slain.
    . . . .
REVENGE: Thou talk'st of harvest when the corn is green:
    The end is crown of every work well done.

                        (2.6.1–3, 7–8)

Revenge has fallen asleep by the end of the long act 3 (a disarming bit of self-mockery by the dramatist?), and Andrea is in a lather to wake him up, for he is completely gulled when Hieronimo turns the tables by gulling Lorenzo about the wedding play:

    Hieronimo with Lorenzo is join'd in league
    And intercepts our passage to revenge:
    Awake, Revenge, or we are woe-begone!
    . . . .
REVENGE: . . . Content thyself, Andrea; though I sleep,
    Yet is my mood soliciting their souls:
    Sufficeth thee that poor Hieronimo
    Cannot forget his son Horatio.
    Nor dies Revenge although he sleep awhile.

                 (3.15.15–17, 19–23)

These choruses, playful in a delightful way, provide at the same time interesting formulations about the dramatic movement. The accomplishment of the plot is a reversal ("love to . . . hate") which comes about by the growth ("harvest" after "the corn is green") of a motive ("my mood soliciting their souls") even though it may go underground ("sleep awhile").

Kyd skillfully provides circumstantial reasons for the delay of Hieronimo's revenge. At first he does not know who the murderers are, then he distrusts (quite reasonably) a letter from Belimperia telling the facts. Finally he learns them from a letter found on one of Lorenzo's base confederates, Pedringano, after he has been executed, according to Lorenzo's plan, for killing the other. To keep Pedringano quiet until the moment the hangman *"turns him off"* (3.6.105, s.d.), Lorenzo contrives that his page hold and keep pointing to an empty box which Pedringano, swaggering to the last, assumes contains his pardon. This "practice" is as clever as anything Marlowe contrived for *The Jew of Malta* and exploits the same sort of relish in ruthlessness fused with our pleasure in theatrical foreknowledge. The Machiavel treats simple Prince Balthazar to statements of "policy" such as "Our greatest ills we least mistrust, my lord, / And inexpected harms do hurt us most" (3.4.4–5). He enjoys menacing double entendres, as when he engages Pedringano to murder Serberine: "When things shall alter, as I hope they will, / Then shall thou mount for this" (3.2.92–93). He congratulates himself on "the complot . . . of all these practices" (3.2.100–101), gloating that "no man knows it was my reaching fatch" (3.4.46)—and then inadvertently brings about the discovery where he least mistrusts! The tables are turned when Hieronimo is asked to furnish "a show" or "pleasing motion" (*sic!*) for the wedding:

> HIERONIMO: Is this all?
> BALTHAZAR: Ay, this is all.
> HIERONIMO: Why then I'll fit you . . .
> $\qquad$ (4.1.68–70)

Eliot put Hieronimo's menacing promise of accommodation at the end of *The Waste Land* and made it famous. In Eliot's context, the allusion to Hieronimo conveys the incompleteness of the response at which his poem has arrived to the latent religious need tormenting the waste land: the outrage to expectations of a sanctified society is sustained, even though there remains the possibility of restoration suggested by "Give   Sympathize   Control." In the context of *The Spanish Tragedy*, "Why then I'll fit you" concentrates all the feeling of outrage to sanctified social values by summarizing the hero's final response, after pleas and protests and mad delusions are over. It says covertly "I'll give you what you deserve," along with the surface "I'll give you what you need" and a further suggestion, "I am joining in the games you play." With the desperate tribute virtue pays to villainy in revenge, the victim has identified with the aggressor, has become in his turn the Machiavel. Kyd's control of theatrical context and language in such remarks can be stunning.

The sense of pressure produced by moral desperation, which made "Why then Ile fit you. Hieronymo's mad againe" two of the fragments shored up against ruin at the close of *The Waste Land,* is the element of *The Spanish Tragedy* that fascinated Elizabethan audiences and that opened up great possibilities that Shakespeare in particular developed. Such pressure is made intolerable for Hieronimo: the closing off of forms of action and meaning sanctioned by the society that has shaped his expectations drives him toward the Senecan underworld:

> HIERONIMO: Where shall I run to breathe abroad my woes,
> My woes, whose weight hath wearied the earth?
> Or mine exclaims, that have surcharg'd the air
> With ceaseless plaints for my deceased son?
>
> . . . .
>
> Yet still tormented is my tortur'd soul
> With broken sighs and restless passions
> That winged mount, and, hovering in the air,
> Beat at the windows of the brightest heavens,
> Soliciting for justice and revenge:
> But they are plac'd in those empyreal heights
> Where, countermur'd with walls of diamond,
> I find the place impregnable, and they
> Resist my woes, and give my words no way.
>
> (3.7.1–4, 10–18)

A parallel in Spenser can serve to recall the vision of an intact religious universe which animates Hieronimo's frustrated expectations (addressed, like Lear's, to a *Deus absconditus*). Spenser's hermit Contemplation shows the sight of heaven to the Red Cross Knight after he has undergone the discipline of Penance, Remorse, Repentance in the House of Holiness. By Spenser's sweet syncretism, the standing place for the vision is like the mountain on which Moses received the commandments, or again the Mount of Olives, or yet again

> . . . Like that pleasaunt Mount, that is for ay
> Through famous Poets verse each where renownd,
> On which the thrise three learned Ladies play
> Their heauenly notes, and make full many a louely day.
>
> From thence, far off he vnto him did shew
> A litle path, that was both steepe and long,
> Which to a goodly Citie led his vew:
> Whose wals and towres were builded high and strong
> Of perle and precious stone, that earthly tong
> Cannot describe, not wit of man can tell;
> Too high a ditty for my simple song;
> The Citie of the great king hight it well,
> Wherein eternal peace and happiness doth dwell,
>
> As he thereon stood gazing, he might see
> The blessed Angels to and fro descend
> From highest heauen, in gladsome companee,
> And with great joy into that Citie wend,
> As commonly as friend does with his frend.
>
> (1.10.54–56)

That wonderful homely last line embodies the feeling for a society sustained by heaven which is implicit in the frustration of Hieronimo.

The Senecan netherworld is for Hieronimo the alternative to beating at the closed heavens—*Flectere si nequeo superos, Acheronta movebo.* Freud's bitter-defiant Virgilian epigraph for *The Interpretation of Dreams* fits the movement of Kyd's pioneering tragedy of irrepressible aggression in response to aggression! Hieronimo explicitly considers, as Hamlet does not, God's prohibition of personal vengeance: "Vengeance is mine, I will repay, saith the Lord." Just after his appeal to the king for justice has been baffled he comes on with a book, presumably Seneca, though he begins with a biblical phrase:

> *Vindicta mihi!*
> Ay, heaven will be reveng'd of every ill,
> Nor will they suffer murder unrepaid:
> Then stay, Hieronimo, attend their will,
> For mortal men may not appoint their time.
>
> (3.13.1–5)

But the speech moves on through reflections on the impossibility of receiving justice, punctuated by lines from Seneca read out in Latin, "*Per scelus semper tutum est sceleribus iter,*" to the final decision: "And to conclude, I will revenge his death!" (3.13.6,20).

Imagery of Acheron has come in constantly to express the need for vengeance, as in the first, very effective scene of distraction, where two Portingales, evidently part of the arriving embassy, ask:

> Pray you, which is the next way to my lord the duke's?
> HIERONIMO: The next way from me.
> 1. PORTINGALE: To his house, we mean.
> HIERONIMO: Oh, hard by, 'tis yon house that you see.
> 2. PORTINGALE: You could not tell us if his son were there?
> HIERONIMO: Who, my lord Lorenzo?
> 1. PORTINGALE: Ay, sir.
>   *He [Hieronimo] goeth in at one door and comes out at another.*
> HIERONIMO: Oh, forbear,
>
> . . . .
>   But if you be importunate to know
>   The way to him,
>
> . . . . . .
>   There is a path upon your left-hand side,
>   That leadeth from a guilty conscience.
>
> . . . .
>   It will conduct you to despair and death:
>
> . . . .
>   Within a hugy dale of lasting night,
>
> . . . .
>   where murderers have built
>   A habitation for their cursed souls,
>   There, in a brazen cauldron fix'd by Jove
>   In his fell wrath upon a sulphur flame,
>   Yourselves shall find Lorenzo bathing him
>   In boiling lead and blood of innocents.
> 1. PORTINGALE: Ha, ha, ha!
> HIERONIMO: Ha, ha, ha!
>   Why, ha, ha, ha! Farewell, good, ha, ha, ha!
> 2. PORTINGALE: Doubtless this man is passing lunatic,
>   Or imperfection of his age doth make him dote.
>   Come, let's away to seek my lord the duke.
>   (3.11.4–8,10–11,13–14,19,21,24–34)

Immediately afterwards, Hieronimo comes in with the would-be suicide's dagger and rope, like the Red Cross Knight in Spenser's Cave of Despair or Faustus in his suicidal moment. Suicide presents itself as a way to go "down by the dale that flows with purple gore" to an infernal judge "upon a seat of steel and molten brass": "He'll do thee justice for Horatio's death." Holding up the rope, he exclaims "Turn down this path, thou shalt be with him straight." Then brandishing the dagger, "Or this . . ." (3.12.7,9,13–15). But he pulls back:

> This way, or that way? Soft and fair, not so:
> For if I hang or kill myself, let's know
> Who will revenge Horatio's murder then?
> No, no! fie, no! pardon me, I'll none of that:
> > *He flings away the dagger and halter.*
> This way I'll take, and this way comes the king,
> > *He takes them up again.*
> And here I'll have a fling at him, that's flat.
> > (3.12.16–21)

—and there follows the rebuff I have already quoted, as he calls out "Justice, O justice to Hieronimo!"

In having Hieronimo actually dig with his dagger in an effort to get to the netherworld to "bring my son to show his deadly wounds," and "marshal up the fiends in hell" (3.12.73,77), Kyd transforms into a pathetic comedy of the grotesque what in *Tamburlaine* seems to extend the world of the hero to include the mythological universe. "What, is she dead? *Techelles*, draw thy sword, / And wound the earth, that it may cleaue in twaine, / And we descend into th' infernall vaults" (3064–66). Here Kyd is pioneering the kind of comedy Shakespeare developed in *Titus Andronicus* and perfected in *Lear*—for example, when the need for justice drives the old king to the mad trial of his daughters:

> LEAR: Arraign her first, 'tis Goneril. I here take my oath before
> this honorable assembly, she kick'd the poor king her father.
> FOOL: Come hither, mistress. Is your name Goneril?
> LEAR: She cannot deny it.
> FOOL: Cry you mercy, I took you for a join-stool.
> > (3.6.46–51)

When an old man, Bazulto, comes to Hieronimo to ask for justice for the murder of *his* son, we get similar excruciating foolishness as the dignified old marshal proposes that they go together down to Hades for justice: "lest the triple-headed porter should / Deny my passage to the slimy strond, / The Thracian poet thou shalt counterfeit: / Come on, old father, be my Orpheus" (3.13.114–17). Even more absurdly poignant, a few moments later he takes the humble old man for Horatio: "But let me look on my Horatio: / Sweet boy, how art thou chang'd in death's black shade!" (3.13.145–46). Kyd's exhibition of the process of regression to magical modes of thought, of projection and displacement, is integral within his understanding of the theatrical interplay of language and action: one can see the poetic theater here serving as a machine for exploring limits of the interdependence of society and consciousness.

Kyd also exhibits the investing of a person with quasi-religious significance as Hieronimo and Isabella make a religion of their lost son.

> Seest thou this handkercher besmear'd with blood?
> It shall not from me til I take revenge:
> Seest thou those wounds that yet are bleeding fresh?
> I'll not entomb them till I have reveng'd.
>
> (2.5.51–54)

The handkerchief, brought out at intervals, becomes almost a Veronica, recalling Horatio's suffering in death. So too with the repeated mention of the wounds. Finally they are actually shown when, after staging his play, Hieronimo reveals the body he has hidden behind a curtain, with one of Kyd's tiresomely systematic speeches:

> Behold the reason urging me to this: *Shows his dead son.*
> See here my show, look on this spectacle:
> Here lay my hope, and here my hope hath end:
> Here lay my heart, and here my heart was slain:
> . . . .
> From forth these wounds came breath that gave me life,
> They murder'd me that made these fatal marks.
>
> (4.4.88–91,96–97)

Hieronimo later on speaks of "my life, / Which I this day have offer'd to my son" (4.4.159–60).

Now it will not do to call athletic young Horatio, killed when about to consummate an illicit affair, a Christ figure. But Hieronimo has made him the object of a total devotion, into the service of which his whole social piety has been channeled. And the mode of expression or embodiment seems likely to have been shaped by religious prototypes, here meditation on Christ's suffering and his wounds, from which came his precious, redemptive blood. The curiously inappropriate line, "From forth these wounds came breath that gave me life," seems almost a slip, conditioned by Christian commonplace; it could be read "gave me death" to fit with the following line— "They murder'd me"—and the whole situation.

Another revealing instance of this making up of quasi-religious symbols is in the scene of Isabella's suicide. Isabella's earlier laments assume a divinely sanctioned universe. In handling her response, Kyd gives her a feminine concern for healing and growth and naive Christian expectations, somewhat like Ophelia's, that persist in violence juxtaposition with her sense of absolute loss and her frustrated vengeful impulse:

> So that you say this herb will purge the eye,
>
> . . . .
> No, there's no medicine left for my disease,
> Nor any physic to recure the dead.   *She runs lunatic.*
> Horatio! O where's Horatio!
>
> . . . .
> Why, did I not give you gowns and goodly things,
> Bought you a whistle and a whipstalk too,
> To be revenged on their villainies?
>
> . . . .
>   my soul hath silver wings,
> That mounts me up unto the highest heavens,
> To heaven, ay, there sits my Horatio,
> Back'd with a troop of fiery cherubins,
> Dancing about his newly-healed wounds,
> Singing sweet hymns and chanting heavenly notes,
> Rare harmony to greet his innocence,
> That died, ay, died, a mirror in our days.
> But say, where shall I find the men, the murderers,

> That slew Horatio? Whither shall I run
> To find them out that murdered my son?   *Exeunt.*
>
> $$(3.8.1,4-6,10-12,15-25)$$

But in the scene of her suicide, the dis-integrated fragments of her "outrage" reconverge in the symbolic use she makes of the arbor or "tree" where Horatio was hung up and stabbed to death.

Misunderstanding Hieronimo's pretended reconciliation with Lorenzo, she enters "*with a weapon*" to "revenge myself upon this place" and "*cuts down the arbour.*" In laying a curse upon it, she seeks to make it a kind of permanent memorial, a Golgotha or Calvary:

> Fruitless for ever may this garden be,
>
> .   .   .   .
>
> The earth with serpents shall be pestered,
> And passengers, for fear to be infect,
> Shall stand aloof, and looking at it, tell,
> 'There, murder'd, died the son of Isabel.'
> Ay, here he died, and here I him embrace:
> See where his ghost solicits with his wounds
> Revenge on her that should revenge his death.
>
> .   .   .   .
>
> And none but I bestir me—to no end.
> And as I curse this tree from further fruit,
> So shall my womb be cursed for his sake,
> And with this weapon will I wound the breast,
>   *She stabs herself.*
> The hapless breast, that gave Horatio suck.
>
> $$(4.2.14,19-25,34-38)$$

Here, as later with the actual showing of the body, there is nothing necessarily Christian in the language: memorializing by creating a sacred or accursed place is a common symbolic process in life, including the classical life and literature with which Kyd was familiar. But Christ was hung "on a tree," as it is often put, and Mary embraced his wounded body beneath it. Isabella's "Ay, here he died, and here I him embrace" shapes her situation toward Mary's.

We noted in the last chapter that one can often see Shakespeare forming secular occasion toward the imagery of the Christian heritage, as when the conspirators in *Julius Caesar* smear themselves with Caesar's blood, as if in sanctioning their own enterprise they can enhance its life with the blood of the leader they have slain. It is quite wrong, I think, with *The Spanish Tragedy* as with *Julius Caesar*—but in contrast with incidents from Marlowe's work discussed earlier—to regard the things that are like Christian icons in these scenes as designed to be *noticed* as parodic or blasphemous. What we have in Kyd, as most commonly in Shakespeare, is Christian shaping of an alternative theatrical mythopoeic and ritual creation. As with Shakespeare, such alternative creation in *The Spanish Tragedy* is used to express family feeling in extremis.

Theatrical Vengeance

There is a remarkable consistency in Kyd's fulfilling his hero's desperate need to move from symbolic expression to symbolic action. Hieronimo's repeated efforts to resolve his need by projection or displacement several times lead to physical violence, as when he tears up the legal papers of the petitioners:

> Come on, old father, be my Orpheus,
> And if thou canst no notes upon the harp,
> Then sound the burden of thy sore heart's grief,
> Till we do gain that Proserpine may grant
> Revenge on them that murdered my son:
> Then will I rent and tear them thus and thus,
> Shivering their limbs in pieces with my teeth.
>
> *Tear the papers.*

1. CITIZEN: O sir, my declaration! *Exit* HIERONIMO *and they after.*
2. CITIZEN: Save my bond!

$$(3.13.117-25)$$

The author of the 1602 text's additions, writing when the theater had become more self-conscious, caught this urgent drive to move from expression to action in the scene with the painter: "Canst paint a doleful cry?"—"Seemingly, sir."—"Nay, it should cry." Hieronimo goes on asking for the painter to express more than painting can:

Well sir, then bring me forth, bring me through alley and alley. . . . And then at last, sir, starting, behold a man hanging, and tottering and tottering, as you know the wind will weave a man, and I with a trice to cut him down. And looking upon him by the advantage of my torch, find it to be my son Horatio. There you may show a passion, there you may show a passion. Draw me like old Priam of Troy, crying, 'The house is a-fire, the house is a-fire, as the torch over my head.' Make me curse, make me rave, make me cry, make me mad, make me well again, make me curse hell, invocate heaven, and in the end, leave me in a trance—and so forth.

PAINTER: And is this the end?

HIERONIMO: O no, there is no end: the end is death and madness. As I am never better than when I am mad, then methinks I am a brave fellow, then I do wonders: but reason abuseth me, and there's the torment, there's the hell. At the last, sir, bring me to one of the murderers: were he as strong as Hector, thus would I tear and drag him up and down.

> *He beats the* Painter *in.*
>
> (fourth add., 128–31,145–46,151–69)

The final play-within-the-play provides this need for violence with its proper objects, Lorenzo and Balthazar. Theatrical art turns into life as actors beneath *dramatic personae* are stabbed to death:

> Haply you think, but bootless are your thoughts,
> That this is fabulously counterfeit,
> And that we do as all tragedians do:
> To die today, for fashioning our scene,
> The death of Ajax, or some Roman peer,
> And in a minute starting up again,
> Revive to please tomorrow's audience.
> No, princes, know I am Hieronimo,
> The hopeless father of a hapless son,
>
> . . . .
>
> Behold the reason urging me to this: *Shows his dead son.*
> See here my show, look on this spectacle.
>
> (4.4.76–84,88–89)

Kyd, who is scrupulous and moving in showing how traumatic outrage drives Hieronimo to this drowning of the stage with blood, makes no attempt to find a moral perspective by which to control our attitude toward him in his final triumph: we have been drawn in to identify with him in his anguish, and we are given no alternative but to identify with him now. Hieronimo runs on and on, recapitulating his grievance and his dedication to it, taunting the royal persons whose children he has destroyed.

> Speak, Portuguese, whose loss resembles mine:
> If thou canst weep upon thy Balthazar,
> 'Tis like I wail'd for my Horatio.
> And you, my lord, whose reconciled son
> March'd in a net, and thought himself unseen,
> And rated me for brainsick lunacy,
> With 'God amend that mad Hieronimo!'—
> How can you brook our play's catastrophe?
>
> $(4.4.114-21)^4$

This first long speech ends by his triumphing in the omnipotent autonomy achieved by merging art and life:

> . . . princes, now behold Hieronimo,
> Author and actor in this tragedy,
> Bearing his latest fortune in his fist:
> And will as resolute conclude his part
> As any of the actors gone before.
> And gentles, thus I end my play:
> Urge no more words, I have no more to say.
>
> *He runs to hang himself.*
> $(4.4.146-52)$

The whole defiance is repeated again, after they break in and hold him, with the variation that now Hieronimo refuses to

---

4. As often, one is reminded of Hamlet—here in his elation after his play-within-the-play:

> Ah, ha! Come, some music! Come, the recorders!
>   For if the King like not the comedy,
>   Why then belike he likes it not, perdy.
> Come, some music! $(3.2.291-95)$

Could this sententious couplet, set off like a quotation, be a tag from the original version? Its style is consistent with Kyd's.

speak and bites out his tongue when they threaten torture. It is a puzzling business, since he refuses to speak after he had already told all. Philip Edwards suggests that the 1592 text inadvertently prints two endings; the second could be a revision designed to provide action rather than a long unbroken declamation.[5] What is clear is an intention to go to the very limits of "monstrous resolution" (4.4.192). Pretending to comply with the demand that he write, he calls for a knife to mend his pen and with it stabs the innocent Duke of Castile as well as himself. That there is no intention to limit the audience's identification with Hieronimo is made unambiguously clear by the final chorus, in which a thoroughly satisfied Andrea promises to obtain from Proserpine appropriately happy afterlives for his friends:

> I'll lead my Bel-imperia to those joys
> That vestal virgins and fair queens possess:
> I'll lead Hieronimo where Orpheus plays,
> Adding sweet pleasure to eternal days.
>
> (4.5.21–24)

After the objects of his violent hatred, including the virtuous Castile, are assigned complementary eternal torments in "deepest hell," Revenge concludes the play with a final sardonic relishing of the idea of actualizing theater: "I'll there begin their endless tragedy" (4.5.48).

It is easy to dismiss the bloodthirsty self-righteousness of Kyd's ending as "merely melodrama," "the old crude theater of horrors"—and there is no denying that, in his own workmanlike, symmetrical way, Kyd piles it on. But if one takes into account the structural dynamics of *The Spanish Tragedy* as a whole, centered as they are on fulfilling and endorsing the protagonist's driving need, it is clear that there is no place else that Kyd can go at the close, no vantage available to him for the ironic control we associate with tragedy. On a much more complex scale, the same thing seems to me to be true of the ending of *Hamlet*, despite the marvelous skill with which Shakespeare handles it so as to put the prince in a sympathetic light and to

5. See Edwards, introduction, pp. xxxiv–xxxvi.

put us on his side. In both plays, identification with the hero's alienation has foreclosed perspective on him from a larger sense of life. In following out the violent action engendered by Hamlet's estrangement, Shakespeare produced a "protest" that is much deeper, more universal, and irreducibly ambiguous. But the radically disruptive character of both plays exploits the theater's potentialities for dramatizing omnipotence of mind and the impulse toward such omnipotence; in both there is a failure of tragic form to control this impulse, to see it for what it is in tragic recognition.[6]

One final quotation will provide a useful comparison with the kind of control Marlowe achieves in *Doctor Faustus*. The author of the additions to *The Spanish Tragedy* amplified the already overblown finale with forty-seven lines of outrageous vaunting, following Castile's question, "Why hast thou butcher'd both my children thus?" (4.4.167). Clearly the final scene's extremities had satisfied audiences of the original version:

> HIERONIMO: But are you sure they are dead?
> CASTILE: Ay, slave, too sure.
> HIERONIMO: What, and yours too?
> VICEROY: Ay, all are dead, not one of them survive.
> HIERONIMO: Nay, then I care not, come, and we shall be friends:
>   Let us lay our heads together,
>   See here's a goodly noose will hold them all.
> VICEROY: O damned devil, how secure he is.
> HIERONIMO: Secure? why dost thou wonder at it?
>   I tell thee Viceroy, this day I have seen revenge,
>   And in that sight am grown a prouder monarch
>   That ever sat under the crown of Spain:
>   Had I as many lives as there be stars,
>   As many heavens to go to as those lives,
>   I'd give them all, ay, and my soul to boot,
>   But I would see thee ride in this red pool.
>
>   (fifth add., 1–15)

The echo of *Doctor Faustus* here provides a telling contrast:

---

6. See chap. 8 of *The Whole Journey: Shakespeare's Power of Development*, pp. 237–81.

> Had I as many soules as there be starres,
> Ide giue them al for *Mephastophilis:*
> By him Ile be great Emprour of the world.
>
> (338–40)

We have seen how the ironic clowning which follows these ec-
static lines comments on Faustus's heedless elation. There is no
such control of perspective in Kyd's rampaging finale. *The Spanish Tragedy* is not really a tragedy.

One way to define what Kyd did make is to call it an heroic-
nihilistic play. One can see it as heroic insofar as it is a play of
protest, grounded in a demonstration of the ruthless forces latent beneath the ideal of benevolent royalty sustaining a sanctified society—forces ready to destroy at need the new high
middle-class servants of the state, the English equivalents of the
French *noblesse de robe,* when their rising fortunes challenged
caste interests.[7] It is tempting to use our contemporary phrase
"social protest" here, but misleading, for the phrase implies that
basic social arrangements can and should be altered, an idea not
present in Kyd's play nor, as such, in Kyd's world. If Bertolt
Brecht had made an adaptation of *The Spanish Tragedy,* as he
might indeed have done, he would have had to put into it some
implication of alternatives to the structural social evils it presents. Kyd simply shows the terrible logic of Lorenzo's and Balthazar's interest and power, and Hieronimo's protest at their consequences. As long as his protest remains charged with the sense
of outraged commitment to traditional society, it has the heroic
dignity of a desperate reinvestment of social piety. But the final
scenes are devoted largely to a nihilistic wish-fulfillment, the
motive contracted entirely to the enjoyment of quid-pro-quo
violence, made possible by the drama's actualization of the fantasy that art can become life.

When one dwells, as I have been doing in writing this, on

---

7. In his effort to provide a social background of class struggle for the
development of Jansenism and the "tragic vision" of Pascal and Racine, Lucien
Goldmann argues that the fierce opposition the *noblesse de robe* encountered
from the *Cours souveraines* in seventeenth-century France often played a decisive role in redirecting political and economic aspiration into religious
withdrawal and a tragic view of the world. *The Hidden God: A Study of Tragic*

the remarkable way the theatrical circumstances give license for enjoying such destructive ideas, it becomes plausible to imagine a member of the Privy Council, say, watching the end of *The Spanish Tragedy* and saying to himself, with Claudius in *Hamlet,* "How dangerous is it that this man goes loose!"—and "How dangerous that this new theater goes loose!" One can recall what Sir Edmund Tilney, the Master of the Revels, wrote on the manuscript of *Sir Thomas Moore:* "Leave out the insurrection wholly and the cause thereof . . . at your own perils."[8] Fortunately for us, such censorship seems to have been rare; Tilney was concerned about the reenactment of the Evil May Day riots, an event close to what might happen again in London. But even though Kyd's play is set in a (perhaps deliberately)[9] unhistorical Spain, it is remarkable, in a time when the Walsingham apparatus exercised constant secret service vigilance to ward off assassination plots against Elizabeth, that the public theater was able to take the liberty to represent, over and over again in a smash hit, an author-actor arranging, by a play, to butcher an entire royal line, "the whole succeeding hope / That Spain expected" (4.4.203–4). One remembers theatrical John Wilkes Booth's "sic semper tyrannis" after he shot Lincoln in the theater.

Perhaps the seditious potential of Kyd's art had something to do with the terrible suffering to which he was subjected during imprisonment by order of the Privy Council at the very time that Henslowe's diary records frequent performances of his play. Perhaps not: the Privy Council may not have known *The Spanish Tragedy,* or not assessed its tendency, or not even thought of Kyd as the author—play-makers being as yet little considered, as the absence of Kyd's name on any of the many editions testifies. But it is at least clear that Kyd's association with the theatrical world, or at any rate with Marlowe, was a cause of his

Vision in the "Pensées" of Pascal and the Tragedies of Racine, trans. Philip Thody (London: Routledge and Kegan Paul, 1964), pp. 103–41.

8. Quoted from the transcription (here modernized) provided by G. Blakemore Evans in *The Riverside Shakespeare,* p. 1683.

9. See Edwards, introduction, pp. xxiii–xxv.

being imprisoned. From his later, pathetic letter to Sir John Puckering, the Lord Keeper, we know that as a result he had lost the favor of his "Lord"—perhaps Lord Strange—and had been reduced to desperate circumstances. I quote Edwards's economical and judicious account of the famous episode:

> Another gleaning from Kyd's letter is that about the year 1591 Kyd and Marlowe were sharing lodgings, or, to be exact, were 'writing in one chamber.' Kyd has recorded how extremely un-comfortable this proximity was for him and it had dramatic conse-quences. On 12 May 1593, Kyd was in prison and a search of his lodgings had been carried out. On the previous day the Privy Council had ordered urgent and severe measures to be taken to find and punish the author of 'late divers lewd and mutinous li-bels' (which have been identified with those attacking London's foreign artisans). Among Kyd's papers were found, not libels, but 'atheistical' disputations, which Kyd affirmed to be Marlowe's and which were a cause of Marlowe's being summoned before the Privy Council on 18 May. Kyd claims that he was put to the tor-ture during his arrest (permission for the use of torture had been given in the Privy Council's decree). It is not known how long he was in custody, but he was apparently not found guilty of the libel or of atheism. His lord seems to have renounced him in his dis-grace, however, and, 'utterly undone', Kyd wrote his letter to Puckering to ask for the favor of his interest, protesting his own innocence and his hatred of Marlowe (whom he refers to as dead).
>
> The last record of Kyd is the translation *Cornelia* (before January 1594). The dedication to the Countess of Sussex is dark indeed.
>
>> Hauing no leysure (most noble Lady) but such as euermore is traueld with th' afflictions of the minde, then which the world affoords no greater misery, it may bee wondered at by some, how I durst vndertake a matter of this moment: which both requireth cunning, rest and opportunity . . .
>>
>> . . . what grace that excellent GARNIER hath lost by my de-faulte, I shall beseech your Honor to repaire with the regarde of those so bitter times and priuie broken passions that I en-dured in the writing it.
>
> This wretchedness is a lamentable end to Kyd's career, for he ap-pears to have been innocent of the crimes in connexion with which he was arrested, and his disgrace was undeserved. If we ac-

cept the identification of Kyd with the son of Francis Kyd, he must have died before the late autumn of 1594.[10]

Kyd's moving phrase, "privy broken passions," takes us back to *The Spanish Tragedy*. For what we have in Hieronimo is a hero who keeps his passion *unbroken* and does so by making it public. The episodes of madness are not the breaking of his passion but his keeping it unbroken.

To put this another way, Hieronimo prevents the injury of the loss of his child from being wholly traumatic. Trauma is something worse than a full-hearted sense of outrage and grief, at least for the individual. It is something like what Kyd describes happening later to himself, like the tearing of tissue in the psyche, so that afterward it "evermore is travailed with the afflictions of the mind, than which the world affords no greater misery." Freud describes it, in his neo-physiological vocabulary, as an excitation which invades the psyche as a wound penetrates the envelope of skin which protects us from more stimulation than we can handle. Such "excitation" can come from within as well as from without, as a result of unbearably intense inner need which in a traumatic situation the organism is unable to master or "bind." We have seen how the murder of his son puts intolerable pressure on Hieronimo's psyche, creating in him an overpowering need even as it shatters all traditional social and religious resources for mastering it. Hieronimo is heroic because he finds a kind of desperate mastery for this need: his power of expression, and finally his drastic mode of action, give form to the vast destructive energies released within him by the potentially traumatic event.

Freud, in discussing "the psychical underworld" of the instinctual life in his *New Introductory Lectures on Psychoanalysis*, formulates in his measured way a principle which fits remarkably Kyd's handling of the Senecan underworld, and of the world above as underworld logic takes it over: "Impeded aggressiveness seems to involve a grave injury. It really seems as though it is necessary for us to destroy some other thing or person in order not to destroy ourselves, in order to guard against

10. Ibid., pp. xx–xxi.

the impulsion to self-destruction. A sad disclosure indeed for the moralist!"[11] There are civilized ways to escape this doom—among them tragedy and comedy. But *The Spanish Tragedy* ends with Hieronimo wholeheartedly destroying those who have impeded his aggression and also consummating "the impulsion to self-destruction." Kyd's play is certainly "a sad disclosure for the moralist!" We resist its invitation to participate in its protagonist's final murderous outrage: I imagine it would be very difficult to stage the final scene for a modern audience without their protecting themselves by laughing at the whole thing as melodrama. An Elizabethan audience was clearly much tougher than we are, or tough in ways that are (or at any rate were) alien to us—witness their attendance at public executions. But if we resist, by moral reaction or laughter, total identification with Hieronimo in the finale, we do identify with his desperate self-expression before the end, and respect it, despite its outrageousness, not only as a human response to shattering evil, but also because we recognize it as his protection of his integrity.

11. *Standard Edition*, 22:105.

Index